MICHAEL HARDING

The Christian Response to Abortion
An Unapologetically Biblical Approach to Abolishing Preborn Homicide

Copyright © 2024 by Michael Harding

All rights reserved. No part of this publication may be reproduced, stored or transmitted in any form or by any means, electronic, mechanical, photocopying, recording, scanning, or otherwise without written permission from the publisher. It is illegal to copy this book, post it to a website, or distribute it by any other means without permission.

Michael Harding has no responsibility for the persistence or accuracy of URLs for external or third-party Internet Websites referred to in this publication and does not guarantee that any content on such Websites is, or will remain, accurate or appropriate.

Scripture quotations are from the ESV® Bible (The Holy Bible, English Standard Version®), copyright © 2001 by Crossway, a publishing ministry of Good News Publishers. Used by permission. All rights reserved.

First edition

Editing by Sarah Ascol & Emily Harding
Cover art by Ricky & Eleanor Doss

This book was professionally typeset on Reedsy.
Find out more at reedsy.com

Dedicated to the generations, nations, and ultimately the millions of preborn babies murdered under our watch.

Contents

Endorsements	ii
Acknowledgments	iv
Foreword	vi
Introduction	ix
1 By What Standard Will We Fight?	1
2 We Have Been Duped!	12
3 Still Unconvinced?	21
4 No, She is Not a Victim	34
5 A Message for the Murderer	42
6 Getting Our Definitions Straight on Abortion	48
7 Preborn Babies Are Full Image Bearers of God From...	55
8 Defining the Biblical Response	69
9 We Stand With a Great Cloud of Witnesses	83
10 What About Exceptions for the Life of the Mother?	93
11 Where the Rubber Meets the Road	98
12 A Letter to the Christian Legislator	105
13 Conclusion	108
Appendix A - "Answers to Abortion Arguments" by Joel Beeke	110
Appendix B - A Biblical Resolution for the Abolition of All...	117
Appendix C - A Biblical Argument for Equal Protection in...	119
Appendix D - "What About Ectopic Pregnancies?" by Dusty...	121
Appendix E - Dublin Declaration on Maternal Healthcare	128
About the Author	129
Also by Michael Harding	130

Endorsements

In one generation, the response to abortion went from "it should be rare" to "it's our right." It went from "abortion should be safe, legal and rare," to "just do it." This kind of sneaker brand ideology has deceived many and distorted the Christian response. As a result, Christians have forsaken the responsibility to be their pre-born brother's keeper.

With a pastor's heart, Mike Harding reminds the church that the blood of little Abel's and Abeline's still cries out. He has put together a faithful, gracious and reasoned response to the issue of abortion. In the midst of this wicked generation, our response must be rooted in biblical truth rather than political affiliation, family preservation or even personal preference.

The routine killing of little boys and girls in the womb has sadly become common and as normal as a check-up. It has been used as a political bargaining chip at the table of justice. This book defines the justice that must be proclaimed and served for all our preborn neighbors. The only acceptable response is love. Love that will respond in rescuing the millions of neighbors being led to the slaughter.

As a pastor, I look forward to using this book to help those under my care not only to think through the issue of abortion, but also respond with Christlike faithfulness. May God be pleased to use this timely and welcomed resource to prepare a generation and save generations to come.

-Mark Hamilton, Pastor at Faithful Stones Church in Buffalo, NY

Michael seeks to persuade readers with a gentle, yet powerfully compelling argument that is captive to the Word of God, which is refreshing in our contemporary debates over abortion. I urge every Christian to approach this book with a teachable posture. Consider Michael's handling of God's authoritative, eternal Word. Listen with an ear open to God's instruction and I am confident you will hold to the convictions of

his conclusion.
-Andrew Hancock, Lead Pastor at Allison Avenue Baptist Church in Hamilton, Ohio

In the midst of a multitude of voices giving counsel on the issue of abortion, Michael Harding redirects the Church and the legislator to the supreme and foundational counsel: the Word of God. Harding makes a passionate plea for the Church and the legislator to harken unto the voice of God, while formulating a response to the contemporary holocaust of abortion. In doing so, he sets forth God's immutable standards of equal justice and impartiality as the banner under which Church and legislator must march, and impressively demonstrates that this has indeed been the case for the Historic Church until the last century. With this work, and the array of resources included in it, readers will feel thoroughly equipped, challenged, and impassioned to love their preborn neighbors to a greater degree of faithfulness.
-Nicholas Kallis, Executive Director of End Abortion Ohio

"The Christian Response to Abortion" presents a full-proof biblical case for abolishing abortion. From beginning to end, Michael addresses every question one could have regarding abortion and how we should go about defeating it. By the end, all excuses to compromise on this issue have been removed. He truly challenges the reader to view this issue strictly from the lens of scripture. Abortion is the modern-day holocaust that our nation must repent of and this book helps move us closer to that happening. This is a book that needs to be placed in the hands of every pastor in America!
-Lizzie Marbach, Conservative Activist

[This book] is a timely, convicting, biblical, Christ-saturated and thorough treatment on this terrible and tragic but, sad to say, culturally-accepted practice in our day. It should be helpful to Christians and non-Christians alike to refine their thinking in seeing the horrors of abortion, a subject on which God is not silent.
-Donald Reisinger, Forgiven Sinner

Acknowledgments

I want to thank, first and foremost, the Lord Jesus Christ, who gave us His perfect and inspired Word by which we can know how to address child sacrifice in our land. Jesus, this is for Your glory!

Second, I would like to say "thank you" to my wife, Emily; without your willingness to let me toil on this project and your mad grammar/editing skills, this book would have never happened. I would like to thank both of my daughters, Joanna and Hannah, for supporting me in this endeavor and sacrificing some daddy time to let me work on this project.

I want to say "thank you" to a special group of people whom I have had the honor of pastoring: Stephen, Carrie, Reuben, Asher, and Jemima Castleberry; Susan Curtis; Aaron, Rebekah, Wesley, Eloise, Evelyn, and Julianne Gerber; Matthew Stonebrook; Chuck and Kay Tibbs; and Josh, Stephanie, and Jackson Witry. Without your willingness to, as a body of believers, see the need for this issue to be addressed and fund this book by allowing me to use my time to write during my family's transition, I do not believe I would have been able to speak on this issue at this crucial juncture in our culture.

Thank you, Pastor Bill Ascol, for mentoring me in this battle for the preborn and encouraging me to write this book. Thank you for the many hours spent encouraging me and sharing wisdom with me after legislator meetings or SBC meetings that didn't go well. I also want to thank Pastor Mark Hamilton, a good friend and faithful brother. Thank you for being a dedicated reader of the rough, rough, and rough draft. Your faithful witness has encouraged me greatly. I say thanks to Pastor Andrew Hancock for your friendship, encouragement, and wisdom in the writing of this book.

Thank you, Ricky and Eleanor Doss, for being faithful friends who have encouraged us in this endeavor and for designing the book cover.

Thank you, Sarah Ascol, for your awesome editing skills and thoughtful insights during the proofreading and editing phase.

I want to thank AJ Reyes for your willingness to put together a preorder / ordering page for this book merely because you believe in its importance.

I want to thank Alvin Hazelton for marketing this book because you believe in the importance of this public conversation and mission.

I also want to say a special thanks to the team at End Abortion Ohio: Austin Beigel and Nicholas Kallis. Your willingness to keep pressing on and meeting with legislators long after my absence is making a huge difference in educating not only the legislators but also the church. "The duty belongs to us, but the results belong to God." Stay faithful, dear brothers.

I would like to thank Bonnie Coffey Cannone, the founder of Abolish Abortion Florida, for agreeing to let me share her story. May God get the glory.

There are so many people to whom I am deeply indebted, and for fear of leaving someone out, I say "thank you" from the bottom of my heart to you all. I love you all very much, and it is my earnest prayer that this book acts as a catalyst for biblical transformation in the way we engage the preborn baby holocaust that has stained our nation. Let us never cease to strive until the preborn baby has the same protections under the law as any born person.

Foreword

One of my favorite coffee mugs has a powerful and piercing tag line which reads: "Every age has its evils; every age has its abolitionists." It was the evil of chattel slavery in the nineteenth century that gave rise to the slavery abolitionist movement in England and America, led by William Wilberforce and Willam Lloyd Garrison, respectively. Their efforts, as well as those of others who joined their noble cause, resulted in chattel slavery being abolished on both the European and North American continents.

Like circumstances in the nineteenth century, the twenty-first century has its evils—the chief evil being the premeditated homicide of scores of millions of preborn human beings in the wombs of their mothers, otherwise known as abortion. And like the days of chattel slavery, the Lord has raised up a growing number of voices calling for the abolition of abortion. Michael Harding is one of those voices, and with the publication of this book, he has made himself one of the leading voices in demanding the immediate abolition of abortion, without exception or compromise.

Abortion has been called "the American holocaust," and rightfully so. Since the wicked 1973 United States Supreme Court decision famously known as "Roe v. Wade," more than sixty million little preborn human beings have been the victims of abortion. This nation is awash in the blood of innocent babies, whose only "crime" was their gestational growth in the womb of women who decided they did not want to allow them to experience the blessing of being born.

Michael Harding's book, "The Christian Response to Abortion" (aptly subtitled, "An Unapologetically Biblical Approach to Abolishing Preborn Homicide"), sets forth in clear and unmistakable ways that abortion is a violation of the Sixth Commandment ("You shall not murder") and places any nation that practices it under the divine judgment of God. Harding challenges anyone who considers himself/herself to be a follower of Jesus Christ to be sure of the standard that must guide us as we work and pray to see the evil of child sacrifice (i.e., abortion) abolished throughout this nation and even the world. He exposes the damnable lie of the "two victim narrative" which is espoused by "pro-life" pastors, politicians, and organizations. In addition to this, the chapter titles of this book reveal that the author goes to great pains to "slay hip and thigh" the various lies and euphemisms spread by the pro-abortion advocates and their unlikely allies in the pro-life industry.

When the reader finishes this book, two questions will need to be asked and answered. First, "Given the valuable information set forth in this book, why would anyone hesitate to align with abortion abolitionists to stop the slaughter of innocent, preborn babies?" Second, "Am I a convinced, convicted abortion abolitionist, praying and laboring for the complete and total abolition of abortion immediately without exception or compromise?"

Michael Harding is a military combat veteran, who fought to secure the blessings of liberty for ourselves and our posterity. He also served as a pastor, possessing a love for Jesus Christ, Christ's Church, as well as all those who need to come to know the saving power of Jesus Christ by grace through faith. As such, he is uniquely qualified to lead the fight to see the American holocaust of abortion abolished.

Prayerfully read this powerful book. Weep over the reality that you and I live in a culture of death, soaked in the blood of preborn babies who have been slaughtered by the millions in the wombs of their mothers. Repent for allowing such a scourge to happen "on our watch." Join the growing chorus of voices demanding that "Abortion Must Be Abolished." Perhaps politicians in legislatures across this country will be variously horrified and humbled as they hear the increasingly deafening demand, unable to be complacent any longer on this subject. Perhaps Heaven's chambers will echo this glorious cry, exciting the angels, delighting the martyrs, and even moving the heart of God to give us the collective desires of our own hearts, bringing to pass the abolition of abortion in our lifetimes.

Finally, do everything you can to get this book, which is a timely battle plan for abolishing abortion, into the hands of everyone you know who wants the shedding of innocent blood to stop. The writer of the Old Testament book of Ecclesiastes remarked, "Of making many books there is no end…" (Ecclesiastes 12:12) seeming to assert that we don't need more books. While there is no shortage of books that fit that assertion, I can say without hesitation that Michael Harding's book, "The Christian Response to Abortion," is a very important one for our times and absolutely had to be written. I, for one, am eternally grateful to God for this tremendous contribution to the abortion abolition discussion.

Bill Ascol
Senior Pastor of Bethel Baptist Church
Chairman of the Board of Abolish Abortion Oklahoma
Owasso, Oklahoma

Introduction

Hello, my name is Mike Harding, and chances are you've never heard of me. I don't have a huge public following. I don't have a radio show, podcast, or YouTube channel. I don't have a Ph.D. in Pro-life studies. Honestly, I am no one special. I am just an average guy who loves Jesus. I am just a man with his Bible and a love for church history, standing on the shoulders of many, many men and women more qualified than I to write on this topic.

So why does an unknown man write another book responding to the abortion crisis in our country? Because the church has, unfortunately, been largely silent on the issue of abortion. I have noticed a disproportionate and unbiblical response from the church on abortion compared to her response to other cultural, societal, and theological issues today. I firmly believe that the church needs to come against this tragic reality unashamedly with the full weight of God's Word.

It is biblical to call for an immediate end to the senseless murder of preborn children. If we believe Jesus is Lord of all, we must be resolute in calling for a culture change. We must also aim to capture the culture for Christ's glory through the relentless preaching of God's Word and the faithful, sacrificial service of rescuing children out of the hands of the abortionist, the legislator, and their own fathers and mothers!

Unfortunately, there have been many men and women who have begun engaging on this issue but have compromised and now defend that compromise vehemently. Believers must stand uncompromisingly on the Word of God. In His Word, we are told that our mission isn't primarily to change minds. Rather, our mission is to preach Christ so that He might be glorified, for it is God who changes the mind and heart of the unbeliever to desire what He desires.

Considering the premise of this book is about ending abortion biblically, my next statement might seem a little odd, but it is wholly necessary to approach the issue of abortion firmly on scriptural ground. It is my conviction that we need to be more concerned with Christ's glory than with ending abortion. Don't get me wrong, I have a desire and passion to see the scourge of abortion in our land end once and for all, but we have unfortunately experienced mission drift. In our zeal, we have neglected to abide within the grounds of God's revealed will. We have made this fight about our special groups and who is in them or about using our approved language. By doing so, we have lost focus on Who should receive the glory. I want Christ to get all the glory for our victories. Ending abortion must not be about our name or group; it must be about Christ's glory.

John Piper wrote the following theological gem in his thesis of "Let The Nations Be Glad."

> Missions is not the ultimate goal of the church. Worship is. Missions exist because worship doesn't. Worship is ultimate, not missions, because God is ultimate, not man. When this age is over, and the countless millions of the redeemed fall on their faces before the throne of God, missions will be no more. It is a temporary necessity. But worship abides forever. So worship is the fuel and goal of missions.[1]

What Piper meant is that the driving factor for missions isn't so much that there are poor people who haven't had the opportunity to hear the Gospel, but rather that there are places on the planet that have yet to proclaim glory to King Jesus. The difference between those who work for the glory of Christ and those who work for their own legacy really is stark: one is God-driven and the other is man-driven.

Let that sink in as it relates to abortion. Our main aim isn't actually rescuing babies! You might be thinking, "Wait. What did he just say? Our main aim

---

[1] John Piper, Let the Nations Be Glad, (Grand Rapids: Baker Books, 1993) 11.

shouldn't be to rescue babies?" Nope, though if we love Jesus, we will most assuredly keep doing that. Rather, the driving force for this mission must be for God to get the glory. It is only then that our mission to abolish the premeditated, ruthless murder of preborn children will be successful. Any other motivation will lead us to an "ends justifies the means" approach so that we look good. This has been our downfall up until this point. We have sacrificed biblical fidelity for convenience and opportunism. We have argued against the sufficiency of Scripture with our faithless actions. This mustn't be so; we must be resolute to speak where Scripture speaks and be silent where it is silent. In doing so, we will be united by seeking to do what Christ has called every believer to do, which is to shine as lights in the darkness by pointing people to Him and His way.

When I sought clear direction on fighting abortion, I first looked to different organizations but quickly learned I had to wade through their internal politics to find anything useful. In this process, I discovered that even though I thought these organizations were, for the most part, meaning well, they were not always responding biblically to the opposition they met, and many were not biblical at all.

Maybe you are like me. You just want clear, biblical direction on how to faithfully sling stones at this God-defying, murderous giant! Friends, God has spoken in His Word and has left no ambiguity on the solution to this social crisis. We must trust that God will bring about the destruction of the cultural Goliath of abortion His way, once and for all, for His glory. When we resort to our methods and maneuvers, we far too often forsake the truth.

God's Sovereign Work In My Life

I am daily reminded of the value of human life as I reflect on my God-given roles of husband and father. I am a husband to a wonderful wife who loves Jesus, and I am the father of three children: one miscarried baby and two beautiful daughters. We are praying for even more children if it's God's will. I feel the struggle to lead my family spiritually, feed my family, and protect them, but those pressures have made me a stronger and better man.

Ever since Christ radically transformed my life and as my walk with Him has deepened over the years, I have put away the old desires I once had to be in strip clubs and sleep around with women. I have done so because I have found my full satisfaction in Christ alone. However, those years of rebellion brought with them much pain and suffering. I now fully see and mourn over the death and destruction that my old life brought. (Rom. 6:23) I have learned over the years that God's way works, and when we ignore it, we make a mess of things. In fact, we typically make things worse than they were before. The Word of God explains the impact of my sinful actions.

In his first letter to the Corinthians, Paul writes,

> The body is not meant for sexual immorality, but for the Lord, and the Lord for the body. And God raised the Lord and will also raise us up by his power. Do you not know that your bodies are members of Christ? Shall I then take the members of Christ and make them members of a prostitute? Never! Or do you not know that he who is joined to a prostitute becomes one body with her? For, as it is written, "The two will become one flesh." But he who is joined to the Lord becomes one spirit with him. Flee from sexual immorality. Every other sin a person commits is outside the body, but the sexually immoral person sins against his own body. Or do you not know that your body is a temple of the Holy Spirit within you, whom you have from God? You are not your own, for you were bought with a price. So glorify God in your body. (1 Cor. 6:13-20)

What Paul is saying is that the person who sins sexually sins against his own body. I sinned against my own body for many years before fully surrendering to Christ as Lord. I even believe that it is possible in my recklessness and rebellion against God that I could have contributed the life of a child to the abortion industry. I will never know this side of eternity, but the thought haunts me as a father now.

Maybe that's you as you read my story. Maybe you are one who still struggles with purity, or maybe you have a story like mine, a story that is plagued with failure and compromise. Maybe, like me, many of your sin struggles of the past have kept you from engaging on this issue with the fervor you should. My prayer for you in reading this book is that you would grow to stand on Scripture and proclaim the unadulterated biblical response to the abortion holocaust. My prayer is that you would grow to desire Jesus so much that the fear of your past being thrown in your face wouldn't discourage your obedience, but rather propel you into further obedience as you embrace Christ's mercy. To do that, you must come to a point of hating your sin, repenting of it, and loving Jesus more.

This is not a book on purity; nonetheless, the connections to the abortion industry are too vivid not to address. Many "Christians" find themselves compromised on the issue of abortion because they refuse to submit to the supremacy and sufficiency of Scripture in their lives. Their selfish addictions help fund the industry or aid human sex trafficking. Let me warn you that the dirty cistern you drink from in your rebellion against God is poison. You will never find life in the temptations you are giving into; there is only death in the soul-destroying clutches of pornography or sexual immorality. The living water you seek, the soul-edifying peace of God, is only found in Christ. Every moment we turn from Jesus to embrace our sinful inclinations, we choose destruction. Even if it may not make sense to you now, the way to victory on this issue of abortion and the way to victory when addressing any transgression of the law of God is Jesus.

See, we come to Christ with all our sins and failures in desperate need of His cleansing. He alone carries our burden. The broad way that leads to destruction is the way of self-righteous action. The narrow way is the way of total surrender to Jesus as Lord and Redeemer. For those in Christ are not lawless any longer; they are those who have been rightly broken by the law and regenerated by the Holy Spirit. The way of Christ is the only way to peace and life. Jesus clearly declared to His disciples that this was the case in the Gospel of John when He told Thomas, "I am the way, the truth, and the life, no one comes to the Father except through me." (John 14:6)

May it be that after reading this book you have the knowledge to engage faithfully in this battle for the glory of God to be displayed in the ending of child sacrifice. For lack of knowledge leads to inaction, and lack of direction quenches fervor. May it be that within the following pages, you are set on fire to preach the Gospel and abolish abortion and are given clear, biblically directed action steps to do so.

1

By What Standard Will We Fight?

"Violence slays its thousands but supine negligence slays its ten thousands."
-Alexander MacLaren[2]

God's standard of justice is perfectly just, and we don't have the liberty to decide if we want to follow it or not. We must look closely at that Divine standard and what is in opposition to that standard. See, to do what God has declared an abomination, regardless of the reasoning or intention of such an abominable act, is to defy God's righteous declaration and act in rebellion!

What has God declared an abomination? Though the answer to this question will be addressed at length in the coming chapters, in short, using unequal standards of justice is abominable to God. To do so undeniably is to sin and ask God to bless sin. Can Christians truly walk with Christ and, upon confrontation with their sin, be unrepentant? Of course not; so why is it that so many Christians refuse to address this issue of abortion biblically and, when confronted, justify their inaction with endless hypothetical objections more akin to a pro-abortion position than the biblical response? They suppress the truth of God in their own unrighteousness and seek to justify

---

[2] Alexander MacLaren, "The Crime of Negligence (Proverbs 24:11,12)" *Expositions of Holy Scripture*, Blue Letter Bible. Last Modified 17 Feb 2022. https://www.blueletterbible.org/comm/maclaren_alexander/expositions-of-holy-scripture/proverbs/the-crime-of-negligence.cfm

their inaction or sinful past actions by paying homage to those actively participating in what was their past iniquity.

Sounds a little aggressive and absolutist, right? Well, that is precisely what God's Word is: absolute truth. It is what we desperately need today. In fact, Jesus Himself claims to be the truth. How audacious of Jesus if it were not true! In John 14:1-6, Jesus says,

> "Let not your hearts be troubled. Believe in God; believe also in me. In my Father's house are many rooms. If it were not so, would I have told you that I go to prepare a place for you? And if I go and prepare a place for you, I will come again and will take you to myself, that where I am you may be also. And you know the way to where I am going." Thomas said to him, "Lord, we do not know where you are going. How can we know the way?" Jesus said to him, "I am the way, and the truth, and the life. No one comes to the Father except through me."

Since Jesus is the way, the truth, and the life, then it necessarily follows that absolute truth claims are a bedrock of the Christian worldview. Since the Christian worldview claims to be the truth, we are not given the liberty to act within a realm of religious pluralism or cultural/religious relativism. Rather, we are obligated to declare the truth of Christ in all of life.

Christian, you cannot claim Christ yet deny that His very words are sufficient for all of life. God's Word is the standard by which we are to fight this battle. God's written law is sufficient for society. There is no other way to bring about true justice other than God's way! For people to deny or delay justice when they have the ability to demand or bring it about is to sin against the person for whom justice is required and ultimately to sin against the Giver and Standard Bearer of all true laws: God Himself.

God has given us a standard for justice. This standard is overwhelmingly supported in the Bible. Scripture screams of it. For the purposes of this book, I'll refer to this standard as the "Doctrine of Equal Standards of Justice." Not only is it exhorted, this standard is exhorted as the only standard from which our laws should be derived. We aren't given the liberty to approach the issue of justice any other way.

Scripture is the foundation on which we build the argument of equal protection and equal justice. It is more than just a "Christianized political theory" that we are asking Christians to support. It is God's plan to bring about His righteousness and grow His Kingdom His way. Because the standard is God's Word, the reality is that we are pleading with Christians to be consistently biblical in their response to the mass murder of their preborn neighbors.

Equal Weights and Measures

> When a man opens a pit, or when a man digs a pit and does not cover it, and an ox or a donkey falls into it, the owner of the pit shall make restoration. He shall give money to its owner, and the dead beast shall be his. When one man's ox butts another's, so that it dies, then they shall sell the live ox and share its price, and the dead beast also they shall share. Or if it is known that the ox has been accustomed to gore in the past, and its owner has not kept it in, he shall repay ox for ox, and the dead beast shall be his. If a man steals an ox or a sheep, and kills it or sells it, he shall repay five oxen for an ox, and four sheep for a sheep. If a thief is found breaking in and is struck so that he dies, there shall be no bloodguilt for him, but if the sun has risen on him, there shall be bloodguilt for him. He shall surely pay. If he has nothing, then he shall be sold for his theft. If the stolen beast is found alive in his possession, whether it is an ox or a donkey or a sheep, he shall pay double. If a man causes a field or vineyard to be grazed over, or lets his beast loose and it feeds in another man's field, he shall make restitution from the best in his own field and in his own vineyard. If fire breaks out and catches in thorns so that the stacked grain or the standing grain or the field is consumed, he who started the fire shall make full restitution. (Ex. 21:33-22:6)

This passage may seem out of place in a book about abortion and murder, but the principle here is that equal standards of justice be applied. This passage gives us example after example of a continual effort to make the offended party whole, even to the point of protecting the rights of a thief who, if murdered, must get justice because the punishment must fit the crime committed. It is only through the equal application of the laws, which require a just sentence for the guilty, that justice is obtained and the wronged made whole.

But we quickly let our emotions distort justice, don't we? In our society, we have case after case of perpetrator and victim alike intimidated by the threat of mob violence, and many are presumed guilty before receiving due process.

In Deuteronomy 25:13-16 Moses, inspired by the Holy Spirit, pens these words talking about the necessity of equal standards and just weights in business deals. It is clear that an honest transaction requires honest scales and equal measures.

> You shall not have in your bag two kinds of weights, a large and a small. You shall not have in your house two kinds of measures, a large and a small. A full and fair weight you shall have, a full and fair measure you shall have, that your days may be long in the land that the LORD your God is giving you. For all who do such things, all who act dishonestly, are an abomination to the LORD your God.

Though this passage is primarily in relation to commerce, the principle of God's law required Israel to use equal weights and measures for their commercial transactions. They were not to rip people off, but rather have rightly balanced scales and weights to weigh people's gold and silver or other forms of payment for goods.

At this point, you may be thinking, "Mike, how does this apply to the issue of abortion?" It applies, my friends, through this principle of using equal standards. Equal standards are not only commended, but judgment from God is inferred for those who neglect them. The passage closes with a strong and very direct warning stating that to do other than what is fair and just in God's eyes, in this case, the use of unequal standards in commerce, is an abomination to the Lord!

God couldn't be more strong in His wording here! The word used for "abomination" is never used to mean "sometimes acceptable to God," and yet we operate legislatively as if that is the case. Rather than operating out of true faith in God and obedience to His Word, we make the excuse that the ends justify the means. We make statements like, "The political reality requires this compromise," or "It's just how the current system works." This is completely backward! We cannot do what God detests and expect His blessing. Rather, if our actions are contrary to the heart of God, as revealed in His perfect law, then those actions are acts of treason. We are trying to play both sides and ask God to be okay with our unrighteous deeds because our motive for doing evil is a just end. Quite frankly, this wrongheaded way of thinking is more akin to selling out our Savior and pinching incense to a false, dead god than it is doing anything resembling righteousness.

Two passages in Proverbs echo what I have already said.

> A just balance and scales are the LORD'S; all the weights in the bag are his work. It is an abomination to kings to do evil, for the throne is established by righteousness. Righteous lips are the delight of a king, and he loves him who speaks what is right. (Prov. 16:11-13)
>
> The righteous who walks in his integrity— blessed are his children after him! A king who sits on the throne of judgment winnows all evil with his eyes. Who can say, "I have made my heart pure; I am clean from my sin"? Unequal weights and unequal measures are both alike an abomination to the LORD. Even a child makes himself known by his acts, by whether his conduct is pure and upright. The hearing ear and the seeing eye, the LORD has made them both. (Prov. 20:7-12)

The New Testament agrees with these Old Testament passages. Jesus argues in His own words against unequal judgment in Matthew 7:1-5. In essence, people can't have differing standards for themselves that they fail to live up to while having higher standards for others and judging them unfairly.

> "Judge not, that you be not judged. For with the judgment you pronounce you will be judged, and with the measure you use it will be measured to you. Why do you see the speck that is in your brother's eye, but do not notice the log that is in your own eye? Or how can you say to your brother, 'Let me take the speck out of your eye,' when there is the log in your own eye? You hypocrite, first take the log out of your own eye, and then you will see clearly to take the speck out of your brother's eye."

Often, those who are caught in unrepentant sin argue that this passage says not to judge, but they miss the whole part that is the standard of right judgment, which is the act of first removing the log out of one's own eye. What Jesus is rebuking here is a hypocritical failure to apply equal standards of judgment! As is often said, "All for thee, not for me." This most certainly is not the Christian position of judgment; it is hypocrisy.

In James 2:1-13 we are told not to show partiality (favoritism) to a person based on their socioeconomic status. Thus, we are to treat them equally as image bearers of God regardless of how much they bring to the table.

> My brothers, show no partiality as you hold the faith in our Lord Jesus Christ, the Lord of glory. For if a man wearing a gold ring and fine clothing comes into your assembly, and a poor man in shabby clothing also comes in, and if you pay attention to the one who wears the fine clothing and say, "You sit here in a good place," while you say to the poor man, "You stand over there," or, "Sit down at my feet," have you not then made distinctions among yourselves and become judges with evil thoughts? Listen, my beloved brothers, has not God chosen those who are poor in the world to be rich in faith and heirs of the kingdom, which he has promised to those who love him? But you have dishonored the poor man. Are not the rich the

> ones who oppress you, and the ones who drag you into court? Are they not the ones who blaspheme the honorable name by which you were called? If you really fulfill the royal law according to the Scripture, "You shall love your neighbor as yourself," you are doing well. But if you show partiality, you are committing sin and are convicted by the law as transgressors. For whoever keeps the whole law but fails in one point has become guilty of all of it. For he who said, "Do not commit adultery," also said, "Do not murder." If you do not commit adultery but do murder, you have become a transgressor of the law. So speak and so act as those who are to be judged under the law of liberty. For judgment is without mercy to one who has shown no mercy. Mercy triumphs over judgment.

No partiality! Christians must be known for equally applying God's standard of justice to all people and themselves.

Equal Standards of Justice & The Substitutionary Atonement

The root of this doctrine of equal standards of justice is in the Gospel. In fact, the doctrine of equal standards of justice is the foundation on which we build our understanding of substitutionary atonement. We can see that in Paul's letter to the church in Rome in Romans 2:1-11. It says,

> Therefore you have no excuse, O man, every one of you who judges. For in passing judgment on another, you condemn yourself, because you, the judge, practice the very same things. We know that the judgment of God rightly falls on those who practice such things. Do you suppose, O man—you who judge those who practice such things and yet do them yourself—that you will escape the judgment of God? Or do you presume on the riches of his kindness and forbearance and patience, not knowing that God's kindness is meant to lead you to repentance? But because of your hard and

impenitent heart you are storing up wrath for yourself on the day of wrath when God's righteous judgment will be revealed. He will render to each one according to his works: to those who by patience in well-doing seek for glory and honor and immortality, he will give eternal life; but for those who are self-seeking and do not obey the truth, but obey unrighteousness, there will be wrath and fury. There will be tribulation and distress for every human being who does evil, the Jew first and also the Greek, but glory and honor and peace for everyone who does good, the Jew first and also the Greek. For God shows no partiality.

In verses 1 through 4, Paul is telling us that people who judge others for something they themselves do will not escape the judgment of God, and that judgment is not merely punishment for the bad they have done but a discipline meant to lead them to repentance for their sin. However, in verses 5-10, Paul explains that because of the hardness of heart of those judging unjustly, God's wrath is sure to come. Every individual will receive the just penalty for their evil actions. Likewise, Paul instructs that for those who do good, there will be glory, honor, and peace. Then, verse 11 is where we make our initial connection with my previous assertion: Paul declares that "God shows no partiality." Contextually, he clearly means in regards to judging both the wicked and the righteous. So, if God shows no partiality in His judgments, then we, too, ought to not show partiality. Let the wicked receive their punishment and the righteous their peace. However, in our society today, we celebrate wickedness, promote partiality in judgment, and condemn the innocent to death.

Paul sets forth that God assesses all people on the same basis. It is one standard of divine justice. That divine standard of justice is most evidently seen in how one is saved from his sin. Paul argues in Romans 2:12-29 that one is not made a child of God by mere outward obedience to commands like circumcision, that one would have to fulfill the law perfectly for this action to help him in his standing before God, and yet this is not possible because all have sinned and deserve God's wrath for their sins. It is by faith in Christ alone that salvation is had. The true Jew, according to Paul, has had the radical circumcision of the heart by the Spirit of God. It is a circumcision of the heart, which is a gift from God, that draws one to repent and believe in the Son of God.

Now, all this only makes sense if we understand that it is the perfect substitute, Christ Jesus, who, on behalf of those who would believe, bore the wrath of God. It is on that foundational truth of the perfect justice of God being delivered by the ruthless murder of His only begotten Son that we build an understanding of justification by faith in Christ alone, not works of the law.

Dive with me into God's law in order to understand this principle more fully. The law of God is reflected on to see the consistent foreshadowing of the necessity of the perfect sacrifice of Christ. It is through the mirror that is God's law that we see mankind's inability to obey the perfect law of God. Then, we understand the necessity of Christ's sacrifice for the unworthy sinner. Without an equal standard of justice consistently displayed by God's perfectly consistent law, the necessity of Christ's sacrifice becomes incomprehensible and illogical. However, since we do, in fact, have a consistent standard of equal justice, we have a basis for comprehending the very pillar of the Christian faith: we are all sinners proven guilty by an accurate comparison between our imperfect obedience and God's perfect, holy standard of righteousness. It is only then that we recognize that we are awaiting the wrath of God. The late Johnathan Edwards so clearly painted that this wrath is like:

> ...great waters that are dammed for the present; they increase more and more, and rise higher and higher, till an outlet is given; and the longer the stream is stopped, the more rapid and mighty is its course, when once it is let loose. It is true, that judgment against your evil works has not been executed hitherto; the floods of God's vengeance have been withheld; but your guilt in the meantime is constantly increasing, and you are every day treasuring up more wrath; the waters are constantly rising, and waxing more and more

mighty; and there is nothing but the mere pleasure of God, that holds the waters back, that are unwilling to be stopped, and press hard to go forward. If God should only withdraw his hand from the flood-gate, it would immediately fly open, and the fiery floods of the fierceness and wrath of God, would rush forth with inconceivable fury, and would come upon you with omnipotent power; and if your strength were ten thousand times greater than it is, yea, ten thousand times greater than the strength of the stoutest, sturdiest devil in hell, it would be nothing to withstand or endure it.[3]

Is it not evident that the whole Gospel depends on an equal and just standard from God for right judgment? We have hope because that standard was met entirely in Christ! For we know that for those who turn to Christ, who, on their behalf, drank the full cup of God's righteous wrath, there is forgiveness of their sin. For God did not withhold His wrath because His Son was the substitute. In fact, it was His perfect will that the Father's wrath be poured out on the Son.

That message of grace is only logically conclusive because God's standard of justice is not unequal in the sense that justice is not delivered. Rather, the wrath of God was rightly delivered with immeasurable fury on the foretold Messiah.

Thus, Christian, justice is served and sins are forgiven, because the infinitely grievous sins we commit against a holy and just God are atoned for. God's wrath was poured out upon His incomprehensibly loving, willing, holy, righteous, undeserving Son, Jesus. See, the only acceptable sacrifice for the sin of mankind in a system of equal standards of justice was a sinless sacrifice.

The principle of equal standards of justice is a fruit of the very character of God. Therefore, when we fail to provide equal standards of justice or do that which is inconsistent with it, we distort the very character of God that is on

---

[3] Jonathan Edwards, "Sinners in the Hands of an Angry God," Blue Letter Bible, July 8, 1741, https://www.blueletterbible.org/Comm/edwards_jonathan/Sermons/Sinners.cfm.

full display through its righteous application.

By now, you know that this doctrine isn't something I am making up; this doctrine leaps off the pages of Scripture in the application of God's righteous law. Will you seek God's direction or compromise His holy standard of justice? Will you delay justice when repeatedly exhorted by Scripture to contend for and provide it?

My plea is that we absolutely must stand on God's standard of justice because Jesus is, in fact, Lord now, and He deserves our total surrender to His Lordship! Jesus is either Lord of all in your life, or you have actually declared with your words and actions (or inaction) that you do not recognize His Lordship at all in your life. Will it be obedience to Jesus, or slavery to the ever-shifting, subjective standards of the world? Will you do what honors Jesus, or what dishonors Him? If the latter, I petition you to stop claiming the name of Christ.

2

We Have Been Duped!

"We commonly represent God as a busy, eager, somewhat frustrated Father hurrying about seeking help to carry out His benevolent plan to bring peace and salvation to the world…too many missionary appeals are based upon this fancied frustration of Almighty God." -A.W. Tozer[4]

To our shame the last 50 years, we taught (and continue to teach) women through our legislative actions that it is justifiable to murder their preborn children if life gets tough. Our laws make all kinds of equivocations for preborn children to die at the hands of either the abortionist or the mother. When we allow a law that lets some babies live while legislating the death of others, we create two classes of babies: those who live by decree and those who die by decree. This is all based arbitrarily on their approved age of development. This quintessentially is not using equal standards of judgment and absolutely must be condemned as ageist, iniquitous legislation. No Christian should ever assuage his or her conscience by using babies as collateral, even if it means to supposedly save the most babies! Rusty Lee Thomas, an ardent and faithful defender of preborn life, wrote the following in a Facebook post and later added to his book, which I highly commend to you titled "Biblical Strategies To Abolish Abortion." Brother Rusty argues

---

[4] Tom Wells, *A Vision for Missions* (Carlisle, PA: Banner of Truth, 1985), 35.

against these silly, unequal, and misguided standards:

> Abortion is not wrong because it hurts women. Abortion is not wrong because abortion mills are unsanitary or do not have proper building codes. Abortion is not wrong because abortionists do not have hospital privileges or ambulance services available. Abortion is not wrong because the child in the womb feels pain at a certain age of development. Abortion is not wrong because children are wanted or unwanted. Abortion is not wrong because of the need for parental consent. Abortion is not wrong because women lack a certain amount of time to consider the decision to murder their baby. Abortion is not wrong because of the unavailability of seeing an ultrasound. Abortion is not wrong because of not properly disposing of a baby's remains. Abortion is not wrong because we can detect a baby's heartbeat or not. Abortion is not wrong because it's sexist to abort an unwanted gender. Abortion is not wrong because a baby is handicapped or has Down syndrome. Abortion is not wrong because adoption is a better option. ABORTION IS WRONG BECAUSE IT VIOLATES GOD'S HOLY COMMANDMENT, "THOU SHALL NOT MURDER!" ABORTION IS WRONG BECAUSE IT DESECRATES THE IMAGE-BEARERS OF CHRIST! ABORTION IS WRONG BECAUSE IT VIOLATES OUR FOUNDING DOCUMENTS AS AMERICANS! ABORTION IS WRONG BECAUSE IT BETRAYS THE SACRED TRUST OF CIVIL GOVERNMENT![5]

We would have endured 50 years of Roe v. Wade in January of 2023 had it not been overturned in June of 2022. Many rightly celebrated the overturning because there is now one less hurdle to abolishing abortion once and for all. However, in another respect, there really isn't much to celebrate because

---

[5] Rusty Lee Thomas, *Biblical Strategies to Abolish Abortion* (Murrells Inlet, SC: Covenant Books, Inc., 2022), 25–26.

there were unequal standards of justice used. Hold on before you cast your stones; I'm not a pessimist (actually, I'm a historical optimist, but I'll save that for another book). However, what many have deemed a "pro-life victory" is nothing more than smoke and mirrors when it comes to real justice for the preborn baby.

The Supreme Court failed to provide true justice and did not recognize the personhood of the preborn child. You might be tempted at this point to say, "But Mike, it's still a win, right?" Not in the way many had hoped it would be. By failing to recognize that the baby in the womb is a person from conception, their decision, though pragmatically appealing, was iniquitous.

For nearly 50 years, the play to run was to get enough pro-life Supreme Court justices in place to finally give justice. I disagree with this play because the initial ruling was not the law of the land. Governors, state house representatives, and state senators always had the authority to defy Roe. This move to submit to the Supreme Court's unjust, unconstitutional rule moved our finish line goal from immediate and total abolition of the holocaust in our land (mass prenatal homicide) to merely the overturning of Roe v. Wade.

So is kicking the can down the proverbial road to the states and equivocating on the question of the personhood of the preborn baby the best we can do? This is not God's righteous standard of judgment. This is not using equal weights and measures! When you disciple people that abortion is acceptable in some cases based on arbitrary gestational timelines, you eliminate the abolition of it altogether and ultimately equivocate and compromise on the issue.

For far too long, good Bible-believing Christians have been confused, and they have failed to closely study the Bible on the issue of abortion. I would also argue they have failed to study the Bible closely on God's standard of justice.

We were all told by the elites in the pro-life movement that we had to settle on the issue of abortion for what was most likely to be successful in the courts, and thus, we should accept the incremental steps they arbitrarily chose. At the same time, the courts pushed objective truth to the side and assumed to be operating from a mystical place of "neutrality." What have the courts ever given us when they have done this? Neutrality is a myth, and we all know it! It is complete absurdity to continue to operate within this framework of fake non-bias. We all have biases, and necessarily so! As I mentioned earlier, Christians stand on the objective truth claim that God's Word is truth, and Jesus is the only way to be right with the Father. He is the truth, the life, and the way! By claiming to follow Christ as Lord, we are saying that we cling to an objective moral standard established by Christ. I labored that standard at the beginning of Chapter 1; it is the doctrine of Equal Standards of Justice.

The late Francis Schaeffer once said this about the concept of moral relativism and neutrality:

> If there is no absolute moral standard, then one cannot say in a final sense that anything is right or wrong. By absolute we mean that which always applies, that which provides a final or ultimate standard. There must be an absolute if there are to be morals, and there must be an absolute if there are to be real values. If there is no absolute beyond man's ideas, then there is no final appeal to judge between individuals and groups whose moral judgments conflict. We are merely left with conflicting opinions...There is a sad myth going around today - the myth of neutrality. According to this myth, the secular world gives every point of view an equal chance to be heard. And it works fairly well - unless you are a Christian.[6]

Did you catch what Shaffer said? The moral insanity that is moral neutrality works well if you have no objective standard of truth. However, those who claim to be followers of Jesus irrefutably do have this standard; we cannot submit to such a foolish worldview of believing there is a place of neutrality and call ourselves Christians. Insofar as our courts keep endorsing godlessness, we will continue to see our rights stripped away. However, our hope as Christians is not ultimately in the courts.

---

[6] Francis A Schaeffer, *The Complete Works of Francis A. Schaeffer: A Christian Worldview.* (Westchester, Ill.: Crossway Books, 1985).

Based on the evidence I have presented from God's Word, are we not bound by God's Word to demand total and immediate abolition of abortion? If we never demand it, haven't we just accepted that abortion will always continue?

The late Fredrick Douglass spoke the following wise words on August 3, 1857, in his "West India Emancipation Speech" in Canandaigua, New York. Though contextually his words have nothing to do with abortion, they have everything to do with the plight of a sector of mankind that was also seen as less than human.

> Power concedes nothing without a demand. It never did and it never will. Find out just what any people will quietly submit to and you have found out the exact measure of injustice and wrong which will be imposed upon them, and these will continue till they are resisted with either words or blows, or with both. The limits of tyrants are prescribed by the endurance of those whom they oppress.[7]

Many have thought, and continue to think, that they had to accept what the courts hold up, though deep down, every believer knows that the biblical answer to the mass murder of any people is immediate abolition. Somewhere along the line, many of us adopted a "whatever will slow the murders" mentality.

However, in that adoption, the goal line was shifted to never truly ending abortion. It also has, unfortunately, turned into opposition against the demand for immediate justice for our preborn neighbor because many charlatans have set themselves up well financially on the blood and bones of the preborn. How have we gone from demanding that the mass murder of children end immediately to legislating where, how many, and under what

---

[7] BlackPast, "Frederick Douglass, 'If There Is No Struggle, There Is No Progress,'" BlackPast, January 25, 2007, https://www.blackpast.org/african-american-history/1857-frederick-douglass-if-there-no-struggle-there-no-progress/.

conditions the preborn murders have to happen?[8] It is an abomination to God, and He detests it!

The Numbers Don't Lie

Here is a staggering statistic: If we are counting the United States alone, there have been more than 63 million innocent babies murdered since Roe v. Wade.

Did you read that without tears?

Unfortunately, most of us do. For some reason, that astonishing number doesn't get the attention it deserves, and it is hard for us to quantify.

Let me paint the picture a little differently. With this massive number in mind, I researched the populations of the 234 formally recognized countries in the world, and, at the time of this writing, the 96 countries with the smallest populations would be completely wiped out! You read that right; entire countries of people would be gone! Here are the 96 countries listed out, from smallest to largest, for you to reflect on:

> (1) Holy See (2) Tokelau (3) Niue (4) Falkland Islands (5) Montserrat (6) Saint Helena (7) Saint Pierre & Miquelon (8) Saint Barthelemy (9) Tuvalu (10) Wallis & Futuna (11) Nauru (12) Anguilla (13) Cook Islands (14) Palau (15) Caribbean Netherlands (16) British Virgin Islands (17) Saint Martin (18) Gibraltar (19) San Marino (20) Monaco (21) Liechtenstein (22) Marshall Islands (23) American Samoa (24) Sint Maarten (25) Turks & Caicos (26) Saint Kitts & Nevis (27) Northern Mariana Islands (28) Faeroe Islands (29) Greenland (30) Bermuda (31) Cayman Islands (32) Dominica (33) Andorra (34) Isle of Man (35) Antigua & Barbuda (36) U.S. Virgin Islands (37) St. Vincent & Grenadines (38) Aruba (39) Seychelles (40) Tonga (41) Grenada (42) Kiribati (43) Guam (44) Saint Lucia (45) Curaçao (46) Samoa (47) São Tomé & Principe (48) Barbados

---

[8] Apologia Studios, "The Fatal Flaw: Lies, Laws, & Pro-life Deception," www.youtube.com (Apologia Studios, November 24, 2023), https://www.youtube.com/watch?v=k33epqzJIlM

(49) New Caledonia (50) French Polynesia (51) French Guiana (52) Vanuatu (53) Mayotte (54) Martinique (55) Iceland (56) Guadeloupe (57) Belize (58) Bahamas (59) Brunei (60) Maldives (61) Malta (62) Micronesia (63) Western Sahara (64) Cabo Verde (65) Suriname (66) Montenegro (67) Luxembourg (68) Macao (69) Solomon Islands (70) Bhutan (71) Guyana (72) Comoros (73) Fiji (74) Reunion (75) Djibouti (76) Eswatini (77) Cyprus (78) Mauritius (79) Estonia (80) Timor-Leste (81) Bahrain (82) Trinidad & Tobago (83) Equatorial Guinea (84) Latvia (85) North Macedonia (86) Slovenia (87) Guinea-Bissau (88) Lesotho (89) Gabon (90) Namibia (91) Botswana (92) Qatar (93) Lithuania (94) Gambia (95) Armenia (96) Jamaica[9]

All of them gone! Thousands of people groups have been torn limb from limb! Friends, do we not believe that each baby is intricately knit together by God for a purpose only known to Him? Yet we have allowed for millions to be taken from what should be the safest place on the planet for a baby and be brutally murdered.

O, Heavenly Father, please forgive us, a fallen and weak-willed people. We have been so wrong on this, though Your Word has been so clear! We desperately need Your mercy. Please, Lord, change the hearts of the wicked. Draw them evermore to Yourself.

Brothers and sisters, I hope this reality is as earth-shattering for you as it was for me. Over the last 50 years, the standard pro-life incremental strategy has cost us the equivalent of 96 countries combined in comparable population! If that is not a failing strategy, I don't know what is! Babies are not collateral to be laid down for our policy achievements and fundraising goals!

Yet here is the even sadder reality: that's just a small part of the atrocity worldwide. If we had to count, the number would be in the hundreds of millions. Since we have not gotten this right in the United States, we have not

---

[9] Worldometer, "Countries in the World by Population (2023)," (Worldometer, July 16, 2023), https://www.worldometers.info/world-population/population-by-country/.

faithfully addressed abortion worldwide. A nation that is morally unclear on the issue of abortion is a nation doomed to fail. If you claim Christ, let me be very straightforward with you: It is high time we fight abortion God's way!

How many more nations will be wiped out in our compromises?

How many more arguments weighing the life of one preborn image bearer over another will you tolerate?

How many more iniquitous, partiality-driven, ageist, ungodly bills will continue to be proposed by professing Christians?

How many confessing Christians will continue to oppose equal protection and equal justice for the preborn baby?

The mission is urgent.

In 2022 in Ohio, 18,488 babies were elected not worthy of life and murdered in their mothers' wombs, and those are just the ones that were mandatorily reported. Let that sink in: In just one of fifty states, 18,488 babies were murdered in one year, and the murderers walked away with legal impunity![10] Yet Ohio is supposed to be a conservative state; its state motto is a quote from Matthew 19:26: "With God all things are possible." It is apparent that Ohio's political process has become completely morally bankrupt.

Florida is another example of this moral bankruptcy. Florida's state motto is "In God We Trust;" yet in 2022, there were 82,581 preborn image bearers of God who were ripped apart in their mothers' wombs, and those are just the ones that were mandatorily reported.[11]

We do not have any more time to decide if we will faithfully stand on the Word of God; the time is now! May we be those who let the Word of God direct how we respond to the murder of our preborn neighbors. Pragmatic ageism has led to the murder of millions. Please hear me, as I want there to be a clear understanding of the Christian's response to this atrocity. The

---

[10] Ohio Department of Health, "Induced Abortions in Ohio, 2022 Report," *Ohio Department of Health*, September 2023, https://odh.ohio.gov/know-our-programs/vital-statistics/resources/vs-abortionreport2022.

[11] Loxafamosity Ministries, Inc., "Florida Abortion Statistics | Abort73.Com," www.abort73.com, 2023, https://www.abort73.com/abortion_facts/states/florida/

Christian's response must irrefutably be one that screams, "NO MORE!" Not "a little more here and there…" No! No more man-made opinions that rob preborn babies of life!

Christians, what does God say? By what standard do we fight this war? I will contend that God calls for immediate and total abolition of abortion without exception or compromise because He demands that we not show partiality in our judgments. Sadly, we have been showing partiality for far too long.[12] James 2 once again gives us more precision here:

> If you really fulfill the royal law according to the Scripture, "You shall love your neighbor as yourself," you are doing well. But if you show partiality, you are committing sin and are convicted by the law as transgressors. For whoever keeps the whole law but fails in one point has become guilty of all of it." (James 2:8-10)

Now that the truth has been revealed, there is no excuse for us to continue to celebrate and promote what God has called abominable.

---

[12] Exod 22:22-24; 23:2-3; Lev 19:15; Deut 1:16-17; 16:18-20; 24:17; 27:19; Psa 82:2-3; 94:6; Prov 18:5; Isa 1:16-17, 23; 10:1-2; Jer 5:28; 7:5-7; 21:12; 22:3; Ezek 45:9; Amos 5:15; Matt 23:23; Matt 7:12; 19:19; 22:39; Mark 12:31; Luke 6:31; 10:27; Lev 19:18; Rom 13:9; Gal 5:14

3

Still Unconvinced?

"In the case of every question of political expediency there appears to me room for consideration of times and seasons—at one period, under one set of circumstances it may be proper to push, at another, under another set of circumstances to withhold our efforts. But in the present instance where the actual commission of guilt is in question, a man who fears God is not at liberty. To you I will say a strong thing which the motive I have suggested will both explain and justify. If I thought that the immediate Abolition of the Slave Trade would cause an insurrection in our islands, I should not for an instant remit my most serious endeavours. Be persuaded then, I shall still even less make this grand cause the sport of caprice, or sacrifice it to motives of political convenience or personal feeling." -William Wilberforce[13]

Maybe you are a person who believes that my argument so far is unrealistic with our current political climate. Maybe you would classify yourself as a "realist" or make the distinction without a difference of, "I am a smash mouth incrementalist." In response, I say that God has not called us to accept the easy or most realistic way in our minds. Rather, we must faithfully demand biblical justice, which is the only kind of true justice and, by the way, is His

---

[13] Garth Lean, *God's Politician : William Wilberforce's Struggle* (Darton, Longman & Todd, 1980), 59.

way! To do anything other than demand what Scripture demands is to trade Scripture for our best-perceived solutions. We are then saying that God's Word is not sufficient to guide us in this matter of life. We are delaying biblical justice and settling for a solution that is wholly unbiblical while pretending to be people who follow Christ! Brothers and sisters, this ought not be so! We must stand unapologetically on the Word of God and demand what He demands. Exodus 20:13 sets our standard for us very plainly. It unequivocally says, "You shall not murder."

Contextually speaking, God knows the hearts of sinful people who are willing to murder another image bearer of God in their anger, and as a sinful people, the Israelites needed direction. It is a very short but direct passage, and yet even many who claim the name of Christ misunderstand its applications. Most people agree that walking up to a person on the street and killing him unprovoked is a direct violation of this commandment. However, for some reason many in our nation support the unprovoked ripping apart of innocent babies in the womb and shudder to accurately call it what it is: murder. The early reformer John Calvin explains Exodus 20:13 in a way I found extremely insightful:

> Suppose, for example, that one of a cowardly disposition, and not daring to assail even a child, should not move a finger to injure his neighbors, would he therefore have discharged the duties of humanity as regards the Sixth Commandment? Nay, natural common sense demands more than that we should abstain from wrongdoing. And, not to say more on this point, it will plainly appear from the summary of the Second Table, that God not only forbids us to be murderers, but also prescribes that every one should study faithfully to defend the life of his neighbor, and practically to declare that it is dear to him; for in that summary no mere negative phrase is used, but the words expressly set forth that our neighbors are to be loved. It is unquestionable, then, that of those whom God there commands to be loved, He here commends the lives to our care. There are, consequently, two parts in the Commandment,

> — first, that we should not vex, or oppress, or be at enmity with any; and, secondly, that we should not only live at peace with men, without exciting quarrels, but also should aid, as far as we can, the miserable who are unjustly oppressed, and should endeavor to resist the wicked, lest they should injure men as they list. Christ, therefore, in expounding the genuine sense of the Law, not only pronounces those transgressors who have committed murder, but also that "he shall be in danger of the judgment who is angry with his brother without a cause; and whosoever shall say to his brother, Raca, shall be in danger of the council; but whosoever shall say, Thou fool, shall be in danger of hell-fire. (Matthew 5:22.)[14]

John Calvin pulls no punches when stating the requirement of the law as it relates to murder. It is not merely for a person not to murder, but it is also to not allow its practice at all. It is imperative that the people of God actively work to stop murder from happening in their midst.

The approach to ending abortion that stems from a "whatever the world gives us we will take" ideology only delays biblical justice. It does so because it relies on the inconsistent direction of the depraved world to define the terms of justice. Never once does God tell us to get our morals and marching directions from the unregenerate world! God considers it iniquitous to do so, and it is using unequal weights and measures. Look with me at Leviticus 19, where we are told our standard by God. You will find that it does not jive with a "whatever works" philosophy. "You shall do no injustice in court." (Lev. 19:15a)

I need to have us hit pause for a second to reflect on this command and address the elephant in the room. What on earth have we been doing legislatively for the last 50 years as it relates to the preborn child? I petition you that we have been doing injustice in the courts under the guise of protecting life. Under this guise of being pro-life, we have sanctioned the

---

[14] John Calvin, "John Calvin: Harmony of the Law - Volume 3," Christian Classics Ethereal Library, n.d., https://www.ccel.org/ccel/calvin/calcom05.ii.ii.ii.html.

mass murder of preborn lives into laws in our states. And what breaks my heart is that we, the church, have, by and large, cheered it on due to our laziness and apathy! For this atrocity to end, we must repent and change direction. In fact, the whole reason Roe v. Wade even passed the courts was due to compromised legislation in Texas that did not acknowledge the equal personhood of the preborn baby. Check it out here:

> When Texas urges that a fetus is entitled to Fourteenth Amendment protection as a person, it faces a dilemma. Neither in Texas nor in any other State are all abortions prohibited. Despite broad proscription, an exception always exists. The exception contained in Art. 1196, for an abortion procured or attempted by medical advice for the purpose of saving the life of the mother, is typical. But if the fetus is a person who is not to be deprived of life without due process of law, and if the mother's condition is the sole determinant, does not the Texas exception appear to be out of line with the Amendment's command? There are other inconsistencies between Fourteenth Amendment status and the typical abortion statute. It has already been pointed out, n 49, supra, that, in Texas, the woman is not a principal or an accomplice with respect to an abortion upon her. If the fetus is a person, why is the woman not a principal or an accomplice? Further, the penalty for criminal abortion specified by Art. 1195 is significantly less than the maximum penalty for murder prescribed by Art. 1257 of the Texas Penal Code. If the fetus is a person, may the penalties be different?[15]

Did you get that? The failed legislative practice of political compromise has cost us more than 63 million lives!

The command from Scripture is very clear and does not equivocate. The command is, "DO NO INJUSTICE IN THE COURT." (Lev. 19:15a) It's not

---

[15] U.S. Supreme Court, "Roe v. Wade, 410 U.S. 113 (1973)," Justia Law, January 22, 1973, https://supreme.justia.com/cases/federal/us/410/113/#F54.

okay to compromise because of perceived political realities and "do some injustice in court." If we are going to be consistent in our view of Scripture, we cannot read into this text the permission to sanction the murder of some babies while advocating for the lives of others. Let's continue on in Leviticus 19.

"You shall not be partial to the poor or defer to the great, but in righteousness shall you judge your neighbor." (Leviticus 19:15b)

As if God wasn't already abundantly precise on the standard, He sovereignly takes away any confusion. When the standard is "You shall not be partial," it doesn't say "except when the ends justify the means," does it? Then, in case one might miss it, we get an even more direct statement: "but in righteousness shall you judge your neighbor." How is it possible to righteously judge the life of an innocent, preborn image bearer of God over the life of another innocent preborn image bearer of God? How is it righteous to delay their justice? It is absolutely not righteous! We must continue.

> "You shall not go around as a slanderer among your people, and you shall not stand up against the life of your neighbor: I am the Lord. […] You shall stand up before the gray head and honor the face of an old man, and you shall fear your God: I am the Lord." (Lev. 19:16, 32)

The standard gets even more plain to see; not only do we see God irrefutably arguing the sanctity of human life, but also condemning those who would speak against the life of their neighbor. I will also state it plainly: Any argument for abortion is speaking against our preborn neighbors, regardless of whether you put the title of "pro-life" before it or not!

Then, to make sure sinful people understand, God seals the deal with the reminder that He is Lord. It is God Almighty who gets to make the standard, not us! And He has indeed made the standard!

Brothers and sisters, it is clear in the general equity of these principles that if applied to the issue of abortion, to oppose a righteous bill of equal protection for the preborn image bearer of God is to stand against the life of your preborn neighbor. And we are clearly not to stand against the life of our neighbor! There is no ambiguity here. So why on earth do some feel they are acting justly to oppose equal protection? I would say it is because of an unbiblically directed and corrupted conscience.

Let us continue by looking at other verses in Leviticus 19, "When a stranger sojourns with you in your land, you shall not do him wrong." (Lev 19:33) This verse might seem odd for me to place in our discussion, but it's important to the doctrinal conviction of equal standards of justice. It is understood here that whether the person was an Israelite or not, he was not to be treated wrongly. His societal status did not determine his value.

"You shall treat the stranger who sojourns with you as the native among you, and you shall love him as yourself, for you were strangers in the land of Egypt: I am the Lord your God." (Lev. 19:34) The Israelites were to treat the stranger who sojourned with them with equal respect, treating him the same as the native. God even reminds them that they, too, were sojourners. They were to love the stranger as they would themselves. God then, once again, seals this admonition with the reminder that He is Lord. Then the unambiguous admonition is made again:

> "You shall do no wrong in judgment, in measures of length or weight or quantity. You shall have just balances, just weights, a just ephah, and a just hin: I am the Lord your God, who brought you out of the land of Egypt. And you shall observe all my statutes and all my rules, and do them: I am the Lord." (Lev. 19:35-37)

We now read the command to "do no wrong in judgment," and that judgment is defined in measures of length, weight, or quantity (most likely in reference to commerce). The very balances that the Israeli merchant used needed to be accurate; the weights needed to be legitimate, not shaved off; and the currency needed to be honest as to its value, not tampered with. This is sealed, once again, by the Lord, but He goes a step further in sealing it this time by declaring He alone is the God who rescued them out of Egypt. He repeats that they are to observe all of His statutes and rules, not merely some, and they must do them because He is the One who gets to set the laws.

How would this apply to abortion, you might ask? The general equity of these principles is true in all matters of justice and personal interactions. By using unequal standards, the Christian slanders the name of Christ and is not above reproach to the surrounding world. We do not have the liberty to set up the standards and laws as we see are most likely to pass when that standard is in opposition to God's holy standard of justice.

As previously mentioned, many have been taught an unbiblical, pragmatic, "ends justify the means" approach, meaning that you can do whatever might work even at the cost of other lives, and even if it is clearly objected to in Scripture. Many celebrate these legislative compromises as if they were pro-life victories. Paul answers this way of thinking in Romans by addressing his hypothetical objector:

> What shall we say then? Are we to continue in sin that grace may abound? By no means! How can we who died to sin still live in it? Do you not know that all of us who have been baptized into Christ Jesus were baptized into his death? We were buried therefore with him by baptism into death, in order that, just as Christ was raised from the dead by the glory of the Father, we too might walk in newness of life. For if we have been united with him in a death like his, we shall certainly be united with him in a resurrection like his. We know that our old self was crucified with him in order that the body of sin might be brought to nothing, so that we would no longer be enslaved to sin. For one who has died has been set free from sin. Now if we have died with Christ, we believe that we will also live with him. We know that Christ, being raised from the dead, will never die again; death no longer has dominion over him. For the death he died he died to sin, once for all, but the life he lives he lives to God. So you also must consider yourselves dead to sin and alive to God in Christ Jesus. (Rom. 6:1-11)

Paul refutes the faulty assumption that because one is saved by grace, that means that he can rely on the grace of God to cleanse him of unrepentant sin. Paul illustrates that the one who has been saved has died to his old way of life and lives anew in Christ.

Unfortunately, the faulty way of thinking that leads people to believe they can sin with legal impunity has infiltrated the pro-life movement. It has been guided by a few self-proclaimed experts on abortion. If their intentions are true and noble, these "experts" are, at best, biblically illiterate and confused. If intentions are not God-honoring, these "experts" are, at worst, outright demonically influenced, money-hungry individuals. Neither of these options paints pictures of people we should be following in this fight against ending abortion.

To be sure I don't get accused of misrepresenting the average pro-life Christian, I'm not talking about the average pro-life Christian who undeniably wants abortion to end but disagrees with or is under-discipled on how it should end. Rather, I am referring to the leaders of many pro-life organizations who have had equal protection explained to them and refuse to act biblically. Those who support compromising God's standard of justice by saying, "We will take what we can get" or "We have to accept a heartbeat bill" (or any other randomly chosen gestational age restriction) are unbiblical. This way of thinking has allowed more than 63,000,000 preborn murders and counting to take place.

Christians who have argued these positions into law have not merely acted wrongly. They also have the blood of preborn babies who have been murdered under their watch on their hands because they had the power to act righteously and neglected to do so. In the words of Alexander MacLaren, in their supine negligence, they are also just as guilty of the murder of every baby that happened while they delayed justice or failed to act to save the preborn.[16]

We are at a point where we need to clearly call it as we see it. We need

---

[16] Alexander MacLaren, "The Crime of Negligence (Proverbs 24:11,12)" *Expositions of Holy Scripture*, Blue Letter Bible. Last Modified 17 Feb 2022. https://www.blueletterbible.org/comm/maclaren_alexander/expositions-of-holy-scripture/proverbs/the-crime-of-negligence.cfm

to call it as God's Word states it; God's Word doesn't mince words, and we shouldn't either. Friends, repentance cannot come if there is no exposure of sin.

My argument to you is clearly not coming from a "whatever works" philosophy, but rather from a "what honors God and best represents a biblical response" philosophy. After all, God has not called us to accept a plan that seems like it is most probable to work, but rather to seek true biblical justice (as if there is any other kind of justice) and walk humbly before Him. We are to trust that the same God who spoke the cosmos into existence is the One who will accomplish His purposes, His way. We are to walk and live according to His standards of justice, not our own ill-conceived standards. We are to rest in His ability to do the seemingly impossible, for as the state motto in Ohio says, "Nothing is impossible with God."

Hey Legislators

If you are a legislator, you may be thinking, "This all sounds good in a church, Mike, but you don't know the House or Senate floor. It just doesn't operate that way!" I humbly contend that we serve the God who gives every legislator, governor, judge, and president their power and authority. He is the One who has seated you in your position of power for such a time as this. If you fail to act, more children will die; the weight of your duty to act should be overwhelming and breed urgency, not complacency and apathy! Christians should not change their standards due to the amount of perceived opposition, dear lesser magistrate. Scripture clearly states that we are to fret not the evildoer. (Ps 37:1) The Christian is to trust in God to bring about the victory in His timing, His way! As is the motto of End Abortion Ohio, "Duty is ours, but the results belong to God!"[17]

Look with me at this beautiful Psalm that exhorts us clearly to fret not the evildoer and trust the LORD and His plan of righteousness:

---

[17] End Abortion Ohio, 2023, https://www.endabortionohio.com/.

Fret not yourself because of evildoers;
>   be not envious of wrongdoers!
>   For they will soon fade like the grass
>   and wither like the green herb.
>   Trust in the LORD, and do good;
>   dwell in the land and befriend faithfulness.
>   Delight yourself in the LORD,
>   and he will give you the desires of your heart.
>   Commit your way to the LORD;
>   trust in him, and he will act.
>   He will bring forth your righteousness as the light,
>   and your justice as the noonday.
>   Be still before the LORD and wait patiently for him;
>   fret not yourself over the one who prospers in his way,
>   over the man who carries out evil devices!
>   Refrain from anger, and forsake wrath!
>   Fret not yourself; it tends only to evil.
>   For the evildoers shall be cut off,
>   but those who wait for the LORD shall inherit the land.
>   In just a little while, the wicked will be no more;
>   though you look carefully at his place, he will not be there.
>   But the meek shall inherit the land
>   and delight themselves in abundant peace.
>   The wicked plots against the righteous
>   and gnashes his teeth at him,
>   but the Lord laughs at the wicked,
>   for he sees that his day is coming.
>   The wicked draw the sword and bend their bows
>   to bring down the poor and needy,
>   to slay those whose way is upright;
>   their sword shall enter their own heart,
>   and their bows shall be broken.
>   Better is the little that the righteous has

than the abundance of many wicked.
For the arms of the wicked shall be broken,
but the LORD upholds the righteous.
The LORD knows the days of the blameless,
and their heritage will remain forever;
they are not put to shame in evil times;
in the days of famine they have abundance.
But the wicked will perish;
the enemies of the LORD are like the glory of the pastures;
they vanish—like smoke they vanish away.
The wicked borrows but does not pay back,
but the righteous is generous and gives;
for those blessed by the LORD shall inherit the land,
but those cursed by him shall be cut off.
The steps of a man are established by the LORD,
when he delights in his way;
though he fall, he shall not be cast headlong,
for the LORD upholds his hand.
I have been young, and now am old,
yet I have not seen the righteous forsaken
or his children begging for bread.
He is ever lending generously,
and his children become a blessing.
Turn away from evil and do good;
so shall you dwell forever.
For the LORD loves justice;
he will not forsake his saints.
They are preserved forever,
but the children of the wicked shall be cut off.
The righteous shall inherit the land
and dwell upon it forever.
The mouth of the righteous utters wisdom,
and his tongue speaks justice.

> The law of his God is in his heart;
> his steps do not slip.
> The wicked watches for the righteous
> and seeks to put him to death.
> The LORD will not abandon him to his power
> or let him be condemned when he is brought to trial.
> Wait for the LORD and keep his way,
> and he will exalt you to inherit the land;
> you will look on when the wicked are cut off.
> I have seen a wicked, ruthless man,
> spreading himself like a green laurel tree.
> But he passed away, and behold, he was no more;
> though I sought him, he could not be found.
> Mark the blameless and behold the upright,
> for there is a future for the man of peace.
> But transgressors shall be altogether destroyed;
> the future of the wicked shall be cut off.
> The salvation of the righteous is from the LORD;
> he is their stronghold in the time of trouble.
> The LORD helps them and delivers them;
> he delivers them from the wicked and saves them,
> because they take refuge in him. (Psalm 37)

For another example, when Moses had to go before the ruler of the greatest nation on earth during his time and demand that Pharaoh let God's people go, the guidance wasn't "do whatever you think will work best," was it? Of course not! The opposite was true!

To do anything other than God's way was a guarantee of God's judgment, not just on Egypt and Israel but also on Moses and Aaron themselves. God almost killed Moses due to Moses neglecting His righteous standard of circumcision. Had it not been for Divine mercy in the form of a wife who understood the urgency of the moment, God could very well have raised up and used another man for His sovereign plan of rescuing the sinful Israelites out of the hands of their oppressors, because He would have righteously put the uncircumcised Moses to death. (Ex. 4:21-26)

The plain, simple, and irrefutably biblical response to the premeditated and senseless murder of the preborn child is to treat the preborn child as an equal image bearer of God and fight relentlessly to protect life by establishing equal protection of the laws for that child from conception.

Will you act righteously and trust the results to God? Or will you neglect God's standard of justice and thus be guilty of supine negligence?

4

No, She is Not a Victim

"Murdering anyone should be illegal for everyone." -Bradley Pierce[18] The woman who willfully carries her preborn child to a mass murderer and shouts her abortion is no more a victim than the unrepentant pedophile who claims he was introduced to pornography at a young age. We must be willing to repent of our sins and turn to Christ, accept the forgiveness available, and yet also accept that there are consequences for the sins that we commit.

    The previous chapters have laid the biblical groundwork for this and the following chapters. I would be foolish to assume that many who read this book will not have already been personally affected by abortion; you may know someone who has had an abortion, or you yourself have committed this grievous but forgivable sin. As a pastor, I have had post-abortive women look at me with tears in their eyes and ask if there ever could be forgiveness for them. My answer is always, "For the repentant who would turn to Christ, there is forgiveness in Him alone." These women understand they have committed a grievous sin. Their consciences remind them every time they see a newborn baby of the sad fact that they willfully contributed to the murder of their own child. This is the lingering consequence of murder. When

---

[18] Apologia Studios, "The Fatal Flaw: Lies, Laws, & Pro-life Deception," www.youtube.com (Apologia Studios, November 24, 2023), https://www.youtube.com/watch?v=k33epqzJIlM. 25:20-25:28

sharing her past sin of preborn homicide, one faithful Christian woman told me that every time she would drive to and from work and pass the exit for the abortion clinic where her baby was ripped apart in the womb, she would begin again mourning the death of her baby. O, the guilt and pain of the tragic murder of such a precious gift from God!

I want to lay my cards on the proverbial table and speak very definitively from the Word of God: the woman who aborts her preborn baby is not a victim. Rather, she is a sinner who has broken the sixth commandment and is in need of the law of God to show her her sin. She isn't in need of someone watering down the Gospel or skipping addressing the hard reality of her sin. She is in need of the redeeming blood of Jesus Christ to cover her. As one guilty of preborn homicide, she doesn't need fake love; she needs real love that confronts her in her sin with the reality of her sin. There is absolutely forgiveness available in Christ for repentant child murderers. But once again, this does not negate any criminal physical consequences for her grievous action any more than the thief on the cross who was redeemed but still bore the repercussions for his rebellion. To state otherwise is to use unequal standards of justice.

To call all women who get abortions victims is none other than an effort to be considered nice and "loving" in our cultural climate today. However, it is actually a heresy that steals the Gospel that would bring her the healing she needs. Calling her a victim is the most unloving and hateful thing you can do to a woman who has murdered or hired a hitman to murder her preborn child.

There are men and women who mean well but believe that the woman is the second victim of abortion. They propagate this heinous lie from hell even though it has been clearly refuted by Scripture, which states that all sin is in need of true repentance. The sin of preborn child murder is no exception to this. Maybe you are one who thinks that the woman is the second victim of abortion, or you have been taught that; please don't tune me out and put this book down. I want to lovingly, but very directly, show you from Scripture and the witness of the church through the centuries that your position is inconsistent with orthodox Christian teachings. But you, too, can correct course and repent for your sin of partiality and acquitting the guilty. (Prov. 17:15)

We must seek to criminalize the act of preborn homicide because God's righteous standard of justice requires it. Saying that the woman who willingly takes her preborn child to be murdered is a victim is like saying that the pedophile who preys on innocent children but uses his upbringing as an excuse is a victim. She is a culprit assisting in or initiating the murder of her preborn child, full stop.

I want to share a story with you from a very special woman who loves Jesus named Bonnie Coffey-Cannone. Mrs. Bonnie was once very much pro-abortion during a time when we didn't have the same technologies that we do now and had three abortions done. She was so convinced that what she was doing wasn't murdering a child that she paid for a friend to murder her child as well. It used to be the case that prior to ultrasound technologies, many believed that the baby in the womb was nothing more than a clump of cells. Bonnie understood the baby to be a potential life, not life from conception.

However, by God's grace, this perspective was radically changed when she saw pictures and videos from an undercover sting on abortion clinics selling aborted baby body parts. Bonnie's story is one of much pain and redemption; here it is in snapshot form from Bonnie herself:

> I AM A "POST-ABORTIVE" WOMAN who has been redeemed by the blood of Jesus Christ. I was vulnerable. I was scared. I was abandoned. I was pressured to abort. The 1st baby's father was a CPS caseworker who threatened to take away my 6 year-old-son if I "caused problems" for him. The 2nd baby's father said he couldn't care less what I did because he had no intention of paying me a dime for the baby. The 3rd abortion was a doctor who assaulted me on the exam table and tried to forcibly abort the baby. But even though I was attacked, assaulted, threatened, deceived by pro-abort misinformation and did not realize I was murdering a human being, I ALWAYS KNEW that I ***ALONE*** was responsible

for my own actions, my own decision, it was my own choice. I decided to abort. I located the abortion clinic. I took the baby in my womb and I laid down for him/her to be torn apart. I would have never DREAMED of even attempting this if it had been legally considered "Murder." When I saw a graphic, bloody photo of an actual 9-week abortion victim, I was horrified and realized I had murdered 3 of my children. I had also paid for someone else's abortion. It was only then that I got down on my knees and begged Christ to forgive me for murdering my children. I knowingly killed four innocent human beings. I am NOT A VICTIM. I am a mass murderer who deserves the death penalty. The absolute BEST way to "protect vulnerable women" from abortion is to outlaw ALL of it as murder—from conception, without exception—and treat abortion homicide like any other homicide, exempting NO ONE from prosecution. We must not second-guess God. He established the Justice System. It is up to us to abide by it![19]

For women living before the ultrasound technology we have now, Bonnie's story was one of reasonable possibility. However, today, it has been well documented that the women getting abortions or taking the pill know what they are doing.

It's clear that many have suppressed the reality of the situation with lies in an effort to dehumanize the baby and justify their decisions. This does not make the decision any less heinous or less sinful. It does not negate the clear malice aforethought that is necessary to murder or seek out a murderer to murder your preborn child.

Russell Hunter is a faithful abortion abolitionist and director of "Abolitionist Rising," which is formerly known as the organization called "Free The States." He recorded a short video on the need for equal protection and equal justice in Oklahoma. He did so because bills being presented in Oklahoma

---

[19] BC Cannone, "I Am Not a Victim," www.twitter.com, February 16, 2023, https://twitter.com/BCoffeyCannone/status/1626390133514682368?s=20.

are not bans; they leave such huge loopholes that never hold the mother accountable. He closed out his video by saying the following:

> There is no difference between image-bearers murdered in the mills and image-bearers murdered by pills. God says, 'Thou shalt not murder.' He doesn't specify which methods of murder are better or worse than any other. And it would be wrong to show partiality to the bigger, older preborn babies and bigotry against those murdered at an earlier stage of development. Also, there is simply no hard evidence to suggest that shutting down the mills has actually decreased abortion numbers. The only thing that has changed is that you can no longer count the number of babies murdered in our state. But while we may not know that number, God does. No, abortion has not been abolished in Oklahoma and it is still perfectly legal in every state of the Union. We are no closer to repentance than we ever have been. It's just that while child sacrifice used to happen in 'abortion clinics,' it now happens in a place like this (referencing a living room or bedroom-like setting). What was once a barbaric practice openly done on altars to pagan gods, then was later relegated to unassuming hallways of offices, is now done even more efficiently and more secretly behind closed doors in living rooms, bedrooms, and dorm rooms. Pills are taken quietly and discreetly, condemning God's image bearers to death. Destruction is happening inside the womb while mothers walk from class to class, office to office, errand to errand, simply carrying out their everyday duties. This is happening all around us while we pretend like the battle is already won. We cried 'peace peace' when there truly is no peace.[20]

So, what does legal culpability look like? If we are to be consistent, we have

---

[20] Russell Hunter, "Abortion Is Still Legal in All 50 States," www.youtube.com (Abolitionist Rising, February 25, 2023), https://youtu.be/XGPv66ZqlEQ.

to understand how far-reaching the law actually is. Another organization that is aiding in the fight for the immediate abolition of abortion and equal protection of the preborn baby is aptly named "End Abortion Now." They shared a great article explaining legal culpability, and I found this excerpt of the article very helpful:

> Legal culpability for the homicide of preborn persons resides upon those that commit an abortion or aids others to do so. Anyone soliciting, providing, supplying, or administering an abortion would be liable. This could be the abortion doctor, the woman, the husband/boyfriend/friend/family member, any/all medical staff, as well as transporting agents (drivers, etc.). All principal actors, accomplices, and co-conspirators would be legally culpable. As is already the case in existing law for born homicide, this would include businesses, corporations, and LLCs aiding women to travel or pay for abortion procedures.[21]

Early church father Basil of Caesarea, who lived in 330 A.D. to 379 A.D., was unequivocal in his call for equal justice: "She who has deliberately destroyed a fetus must bear the penalty for murder. Moreover those who aid her, who give abortifacients for the destruction of a child conceived in the womb are murderers themselves, along with those receiving the poisons."[22]

Zach Conover, Director of Communications for End Abortion Now, addresses objections to equal protection and equal justice by saying the following:

> If we're going to be obedient to the Word of God and maintain a logically consistent ethic for life, we must allow for the prosecution

---

[21] End Abortion Now, "Common Objections to Equal Protection," End Abortion Now, December 13, 2022, https://endabortionnow.com/common-objections-to-equal-protection.

[22] George Grant, *Third Time Around: A History of the Pro-Life Movement from the First Century to the Present* (Brentwood, TN: Wolgemuth & Hyatt, Publishers, Inc., 1991), 20.

of aborting mothers. The only way to provide equal protection for children in the womb is to make sure that no one is allowed to take their lives.[23]

Let's look at how good laws instruct to righteousness and how bad laws instruct to unrighteousness. Bradley Pierce is a constitutional lawyer fighting to abolish abortion without exceptions or compromise. He explains the issue of treating women as victims in an article critiquing the 2022-2023 president of the Southern Baptist Convention, Pastor Bart Barber:

> Perhaps one of the chief reasons many women in our country believe there is nothing wrong with aborting a child is that even the bills pushed by the Pro-Life movement have taught them this. The law is a tutor. When a Pro-Life bill says that the abortive mother has done nothing legally wrong, they believe it. Sadly, the Pro-Life establishment has been complicit in perpetuating this grave misunderstanding. The abolition bills Barber opposes are actually the solution. First, once they went into effect, abolition bills of equal protection would immediately teach everyone that a human being from fertilization to birth is just as much a human being as one after birth. Secondly, unlike the Pro-Life bills Barber supports, abolition bills would actually deal with the pressure placed upon women by their boyfriends, parents, and the abortion industry. When was the last time someone seriously tried to talk you into or pressure you into murdering a born person? It has probably never happened to you. Why not? Because it is illegal! And if you were to go through with it, the person who talked you into it would be a party to your crime. Yet because abortion is not currently treated as homicide in any state, guess what is not illegal. That's

---

[23] Zach Conover, "Responding to Objections against Criminalization," End Abortion Now, January 30, 2023, https://endabortionnow.com/responding-to-objections-against-criminalization/.

right. Because Pro-Life legislation says it is legal for a mother to get an abortion, that also makes it legal to encourage her to do it. And up to threatening her life or limb.[24]

There is video after video of women "shouting their abortion" and pro-abortion groups outright arguing they know the preborn child is a human baby but believe they should still have the right to murder that baby. This undeniably refutes the idea that the woman getting an abortion of her own free will is a victim.

We cannot offer the Gospel if the women who commit this grievous sin are only ever seen as victims. Again, if we call the woman who willfully gets an abortion a victim, we strip her of the need to repent and trust Christ and thus strip her of the Gospel of Jesus Christ.

If you are that woman, though this message is hard to bear, the next chapter is for you.

---

[24] Bradley Pierce, "Abolition and Equal Protection: A Response to Barber's False Claims," Founders Ministries, February 21, 2023, https://founders.org/articles/abolition-and-equal-protection-a-response-to-barbers-false-claims/.

5

A Message for the Murderer

If you are a mother who willfully murdered your preborn child or a father who had his preborn child murdered and have come to see abortion as the sin that it is, Jesus is the answer to your mourning and there is forgiveness available to you in Him alone. The Gospel is for you, too! The Bible is clear that we are all born sinners in need of a Savior. Scripture tells us,

> ...for all have sinned and fall short of the glory of God, and are justified by his grace as a gift, through the redemption that is in Christ Jesus, whom God put forward as a propitiation by his blood, to be received by faith. This was to show God's righteousness, because in his divine forbearance he had passed over former sins. It was to show his righteousness at the present time, so that he might be just and the justifier of the one who has faith in Jesus. (Rom. 3:23-27)

As sinners, we all stand condemned before a holy and perfectly just God. We deserve to receive His eternal wrath for our sins. We are also told that "...the wages of sin is death..." (Rom. 6:23a)

We earn a paycheck of death in our sinful endeavors. This is tragic, hopeless news if one stops reading the passage there. However, through God's unmerited favor on us, the unrighteous, the passage continues with a beautiful, redeeming conjunction: "…but the free gift of God is eternal life in Christ Jesus our LORD." (Rom 6:23b)

Is He your Lord? Have you, in fact, really and truly put your faith in Him? I don't mean, have you prayed a prayer in your youth. No, I mean, have you cried out for mercy and repented of your sins and genuinely turned to Jesus as LORD? Has your life borne the fruit of this? (Rom. 10:13)

It often seems as if when people read Paul's words in the previous verse, they do so under a lens of "I have to clean myself up first. I have to become a good person and then I'll get that church stuff right." But Paul tells us in Romans 5, "…God shows His love for us in that while we were still sinners…" (Rom. 5:8a) Does it say that God gave up on us and admitted our sins were too heinous for the blood of His only begotten Son to cover?

No, it says, "…while we were still sinners, Christ died for us." (Rom. 5:8b)

What do we do with this kind of life-transforming mercy and grace? God has answered that question for us as well! First, we repent of our sins, which means confessing our sins to the Lord, turning from them, and turning to Christ. Then, the second part of this is to confess that Jesus is Lord.

Thomas Watson had this to say about the nature of true repentance: "Repentance is a grace of God's Spirit whereby a sinner is inwardly humbled and visibly reformed."[25] What he means is that repentance is a fruit of the regenerating work of the Holy Spirit in the life of the believer.

Now that we have talked about repentance, we also must talk about what it means to confess that Jesus is Lord and believe that God raised Him from the dead. This is where the repentant sinner turns after having turned from his sin. He doesn't merely turn to nothing; he turns to Christ. The Apostle Paul writes later in Romans 10,

> Brothers, my heart's desire and prayer to God for them [he is speaking of his kinsmen, the Jews] is that they may be saved. For I bear them witness that they have a zeal for God, but not according to knowledge. For, being ignorant of the righteousness of God,

---

[25] Thomas Watson, *The Doctrine of Repentance* (Carlisle, PA: Banner of Truth, 1999), 18.

and seeking to establish their own, they did not submit to God's righteousness. For Christ is the end of the law for righteousness to everyone who believes... (Rom. 10:1-4)

Paul is refuting the foolish and misdirected zeal the Jews had and says that Christ has fulfilled the righteous, perfect requirements of God's law for all who put their faith in Him. Continue with me in this passage,

> For Moses writes about the righteousness that is based on the law, that the person who does the commandments shall live by them. But the righteousness based on faith says, "Do not say in your heart, 'Who will ascend into heaven?'" (that is, to bring Christ down) "or 'Who will descend into the abyss?'" (that is, to bring Christ up from the dead). But what does it say? "The word is near you, in your mouth and in your heart" (that is, the word of faith that we proclaim);... (Rom. 10:5-8)

Paul explains that the works of the law do not render one saved. There has only ever been One who was perfect, and it is through Him and Him alone that one ascends into heaven versus the abyss. The Jews would have known the law of Moses and understood these connections clearly, for the Word was indeed near them and in their hearts. Paul is making it clear that he is not proclaiming something in opposition to the law of God. Rather, he is actually proclaiming the only One to ever have lived in perfect obedience to the law of God. The passage continues in almost climactic form because Paul has been laying the case in the previous 9 chapters:

> ...because, if you confess with your mouth that Jesus is Lord and believe in your heart that God raised him from the dead, you will be saved. For with the heart one believes and is justified, and with the mouth one confesses and is saved. For the Scripture says, "Everyone who believes in him will not be put to shame." (Rom. 10:9-11)

Paul states that if the Jews he was talking to confessed with their mouths that Jesus is Lord and believed in their hearts that God really did raise Him from the dead, they would be saved because they would have accepted the Gospel and trusted in Christ. Did you read that? Those unworthy sinners who believe in Christ, those who put their faith and trust in Him, will not be put to shame! Those who believe in Jesus will not be put to shame!

Continuing on in the text, Paul says, "For there is no distinction between Jew and Greek; for the same Lord is Lord of all, bestowing his riches on all who call on him. For 'everyone who calls on the name of the Lord will be saved.'" (Rom. 10:12-13) There is no partiality between the Jew and Greek, for the Lord is the same Lord of all, and He bestows His riches on all who call on His name!

To those who have been apathetic to abortion, to those who have participated in abortion, and to those who are today mourning it, there is forgiveness in Jesus if you repent of this sin and put your faith in Him. If you are a Christian but have sinned in this area, would you not also do well to repent of your sins, turn to Christ, and trust His ways? There is no need for penance for those who have committed the act of prenatal homicide, just true righteous repentance, and faith in Jesus alone!

It Is a Great Commission Issue

Christian, this is for you. Abortion is truly a Great Commission issue because it is an issue of truly loving our preborn neighbor as ourselves. However, before we make application there, we must also note that abortion is a law of God issue. In a way only He can do, Jesus summarizes the moral law of God into two tables: the first table is the first four commands, which cover loving God with all one's heart, soul, mind, and strength; and the second table covers the last six commands, which are summed up as loving our neighbor as ourselves. (Matt. 22:37-40)

If we really love our preborn neighbors as ourselves, then we have to stop those who keep murdering them. The only true stop to evil in society is the Gospel going forth and creating a Christ-honoring culture. Do you want to end abortion? Preach Christ! Do you want to change the culture? Disciple others to be biblically informed in how they ought to live out their lives. For far too long, the American church has been sleeping on the issue of abortion and the words of Francis Schaeffer unfortunately ring true: "Every abortion clinic should have a sign in front of it saying, 'Open by the permission of the church.'"[26]

Let me share with you this quote from my pastor, Tom Ascol, of Grace Baptist Church in Cape Coral, Florida.

> There is a Savior for sinners, including those who are guilty of participating in the sin of abortion. Jesus Christ came into the world to live a righteous life and die a sacrificial death so that all who repent and look to Him in faith might be saved. His grace is enough to forgive both abortionists and those who employ them to end the life of their preborn child. So while we work for justice to protect the lives of the preborn, let's never forget to preach the gospel that saves even the foremost of sinners and encourage abortionists, those who employ them, pro-lifers, and abolitionists to trust the Lord Jesus Christ and find eternal life in Him.[27]

The hope that true believers have to overcome their past sin is insurmountably great due to an insurmountably awesome God. Jesus lived the perfect life we couldn't, died a horrendous death on a Roman cross in our place, was buried in a rich man's tomb, and was raised to life on the third day. He is now seated at the right hand of God the Father.

Will you seek God's direction, or will you compromise His holy standard of justice? We must stand on His standard of justice because Jesus is, in fact,

---

[26] Dewey Moede, "Francis Shaeffer Holding the Church Accountable on Abortion," For God's Glory Alone Ministries, July 11, 2013, https://www.fggam.org/2013/07/francis-shaeffer-holding-the-church-accountable-on-abortion/.

[27] Tom Ascol, "Toward a Principled Pro-Life Ethic in Post-Roe America," Founders Ministries, May 17, 2022, http://founders.org/articles/toward-a-principled-pro-life-ethic-in-post-roe-america.

Lord now and He deserves our total surrender to His Lordship! Jesus is either Lord of all or not Lord at all in our lives. What is it with you? As for me and my house, we acknowledge Jesus' Lordship and submit to what His Word lays out on all issues of life and practice of our faith.

6

Getting Our Definitions Straight on Abortion

"Abortion is an ethical issue, perhaps the central ethical issue of the twentieth and now the twenty-first centuries. As a question of ethics, abortion is not morally neutral; it does not fall within the gray zone of things that are indifferent." -R.C. Sproul[28]

We live in a world where one word can often be understood many different ways by many different people. After all, we live in a culture where deconstructionism is pervasive as a fruit of postmodernism, and moral and cultural relativism are merely grandchildren of deconstructionism. Let me define a term that is stated over and over through this book: abortion.

Abortion is the unjustified, premeditated killing of a preborn human child; it is, in action, preborn homicide; or, more biblically appropriated, it is the murder of a preborn image bearer of God.

Some have argued that abortion is merely getting rid of a clump of cells and

---

[28] Robert Charles Sproul, *Abortion: A Rational Look at an Emotional Issue* (Sanford, FL: Reformation Trust Publishing, 2010), xxi.

that the baby in the womb is nothing more than potential life until it is born. However, the biological and biblical reality is that abortion is not merely getting rid of cells; it is definitively the taking of a life. It is not taking a potential life; it is stopping a developing life! The baby in the womb is a full image bearer of God from fertilization.

I find myself contemplating how it is that those who claim to be Christians have gotten abortion categorically wrong for so long and have failed to provide equal justice and equal protection for the most innocent among us. I have come to the belief that, in many ways, we have arrived at the wrong definition of abortion because we are a selfish people. It's much easier to rewrite the definition of child murder than own up to its reality. It's much easier to ignore the holocaust than address it and deal with the moral depravity that drives it.

The moral social crisis we are in fundamentally stems from a misunderstanding of the moral depravity that indwells the depths of humanity. Ephesians 2 says,

> And you were dead in the trespasses and sins in which you once walked, following the course of this world, following the prince of the power of the air, the spirit that is now at work in the sons of disobedience—among whom we all once lived in the passions of our flesh, carrying out the desires of the body and the mind, and were by nature children of wrath, like the rest of mankind. (Eph. 2:1-3)

For a true reflection of this reality, one merely needs to stand outside an abortion clinic for a few hours on a kill day. You will witness all manner of perversity and satanic celebration when the blood of an innocent baby in the womb is shed. You will see mothers making all sorts of gestures and hear them using language that would make a sailor blush. Most of the women that I have personally witnessed going into the abortion mill are not victims; they celebrate their abortions. I would encourage the reader to reference the footnotes where I have included a website dedicated to refuting the idea that the woman who gets an abortion today is a victim and is uneducated on what abortion is.[29] The tragic display of complete disregard for human dignity that is so often seen at murder mills should remind any true follower of Christ that Satan and his ways always bring death and destruction.

Now to address the issue of misappropriating terms and ignoring the objectively clear facts of what abortion is and isn't. I do well to remind the reader that the unapologetically Christian approach to the issue of abortion that will be found here precludes one from leaning on opinion. In order to aim the canons of Scripture at the right target, we must first be clear that how we approach abortion is fundamentally shaped by the following: who we worship; what we think about the nature of mankind; what we understand to be sin; and how we understand one is saved from the just punishment for sin.

First, abortion is an issue of worship. If the murder of preborn children is condemned in Scripture, which it irrefutably is (Ex. 20:13), then murdering one's child is an act of defiance against the Creator who knits each child together in the mother's womb. In a culture of death, the unregenerate offer up their children on the altar of pleasure and promiscuity. They offer worship to the zeitgeist (the spirit of the age) and celebrate their defiance against the Creator God with kazoos and clapping.

Second, the reality that abortion is legal in our land says a lot about what we believe mankind to be and in whom we find our image. We are not autonomous, free creatures to do as we please; we are subject to the laws that God has ordained. We are accountable to God for every action we take in our lives and one day we will be called to account for those actions.

Third, in order to correctly address the issue of abortion, we must have a biblical understanding of sin. Those who victimize the woman who murders her child or has her child ruthlessly ripped apart or burned alive at an abortion mill actually steal the Gospel from her. If abortion is not a sin problem, then there is no need for repentance.

Finally, once we grasp the biblical understanding of sin, then we must follow

---

[29] #NotAVictim, "Videos Archives," 2023, https://notavictim.org/category/videos/.

what Scripture says about how one is saved from God's just punishment for sin. If we do not understand the need to repent of our sins, then we cannot rightfully acknowledge our need for Jesus. If we do not humbly come in true repentance of our sins before Christ, there is no salvation for the sinner.

If our definition of abortion is true to the reality of abortion, then the preborn baby is undeniably a person and the Christian is obligated to value all image bearers of God equally. The only biblical response to abortion is to demand its immediate abolition in our land and to criminally punish those who practice it.

Don't Turn Your Eyes

If you have never read how preborn babies are murdered, I will warn you that the following paragraphs will shake you. However, it is necessary that we have no ambiguity about what is happening in an abortion because this is what is happening across the globe to our preborn neighbors. This was the hardest section for me to write, and yet it was the one that drove me to finish writing this book. I wrote this section with a heavy heart. Friends, please don't rush through these horrific details; let them drive you to biblically faithful action.

The slaughtering of preborn children in our day is typically legally done in the following ways, but it is not limited to them; it should be no surprise that evil people will come up with new ways to murder innocent children.

Suction Abortion (Suction Aspiration)

This procedure is used in 80 % of the abortions up to the 12th week of pregnancy. The mouth of the cervix is dilated, then a hollow tube with a knife-like edged tip is inserted into the womb. A suction force 28 times stronger than a vacuum cleaner literally tears the developing baby to pieces and sucks the remains into a container.

Dilation and Curettage Abortion

Dilation and Curettage (commonly known as D & C) is a procedure which involves dilating the cervix with a series of instruments to allow the insertion of a curette (a loop shaped knife) into the womb. The instrument is used to scrape the placenta from the uterus and then cut the baby apart into pieces. The pieces are then drawn through the cervix. The baby's body must then be reassembled by an attending physician or nurse to make sure no baby parts remain in the mother because they would cause an infection if left in the womb.

Saline Injection Abortion

Saline Injection (also known as "Salt-Poisoning") is an abortion procedure which involves removing some of the amniotic fluid surrounding the baby and replacing it with a toxic, saline solution. The baby then breathes and swallows the solution. In one or two hours the preborn baby dies from salt poisoning, dehydration, and hemorrhaging. The mother goes into labor about 24 hours later and delivers a dead or still dying baby.

Hysterotomy Abortion

During the last 3 months of a pregnancy, abortions are performed by hysterotomy. This involves opening the womb surgically and removing the baby as in a Cesarean Section (C-Section). However, the purpose of this procedure is to murder the baby. Instead of being cared for, the baby is wrapped in a blanket, set aside, and allowed to die.

Prostaglandin Abortion

This type of abortion involves use of prostaglandin hormones injected into the womb or released in a vaginal suppository. The hormones cause the uterus to contract and deliver the child prematurely. This has the desired effect of premature birth whereby the baby is delivered before being viable outside the womb and either left to die or murdered at birth. This type of abortion is sometimes coupled with Saline Injection to initiate a pre-birth death process in order to make the killing process quicker upon delivery.

Chemical Abortion

Chemical abortions are not limited to the following process, but they are typically performed this way. In the chemical abortion process, a pregnant woman typically takes two pills: mifepristone and misoprostol. Mifepristone acts to block the uterus from receiving a critical hormone, progesterone, which is required to sustain a pregnancy. As a result of the progesterone inhibitor, the lining of the uterus deteriorates and cannot transfer adequate nutrients to the developing unborn child, causing its death. Twenty-four to forty-eight hours after taking mifepristone, the pregnant woman takes the second part of the abortion pill regimen, misoprostol, which causes uterine contractions to complete the abortion process and empty the uterus. Misoprostol's use in the abortion pill regimen is "off label," which means it was not created to be used in the abortion process. Planned Parenthood documents this as the preferred chemical abortion process on their own website.[30]

We Must Repent

I cannot end this chapter without expressing repentance for the years of apathy I have had; in my many years of rebellion against God, I didn't think twice about the reality of this holocaust. May our nation and the church of Jesus Christ one day repent for her gross negligence and complicity to the mass murder of preborn babies. Join me in praying this prayer:

Dear God, we are a people who have failed to establish justice for far too long. I

---

[30] Planned Parenthood, "The Abortion Pill," Plannedparenthood.org, 2019, https://www.plannedparenthood.org/learn/abortion/the-abortion-pill.

feel the weight of the millions of innocent preborn, fatherless lives ripped apart in the womb. O the agony that these poor image bearers endure, Lord. Have mercy, O Lord, on us undeserving people. Raise up courageous men and women to stand in the gap for the most innocent among us. I am sorry, Lord, for the years of apathy that were wasted in my life, for not defending the fatherless and proclaiming your Lordship. Jesus, You are King, and one day You will put abortion under Your feet and the bloodletting will be no more. But until that day, help us to faithfully oppose Satan and his bloodthirsty demons. Help us, Lord, to take the Gospel to the gates of hell and push back the darkness for Your glory. Give us victory in the legislature. Lord, please bring at least one state to establish equal protection and equal justice for the preborn! In Jesus's holy name I pray, Amen.

7

Preborn Babies Are Full Image Bearers of God From Fertilization

In whose image is a child created? Is it Mommy and Daddy? These questions matter in the fight to abolish abortion. If children are merely a mini version of their parents, then one could possibly make an autonomy argument. If the child has no intrinsic value outside of what the parents arbitrarily bestow on him or her, then we have no dog in the fight on abortion.

However, in the Christian worldview we understand each child as a gift from God, and each child finds his or her value by being made in the image of the Creator from conception.[31] For God's word says,

> Behold, children are a heritage from the LORD, the fruit of the womb a reward. Like arrows in the hand of a warrior are the children of one's youth. Blessed is the man who fills his quiver with them! He shall not be put to shame when he speaks with his enemies in the gate. (Ps. 127:3-5)

---

[31] Gen. 4:1, 4:17, 16:11, 19:36, 21:2, 25:22, 29:32-35, 30:5, 30:7, 30:17, 30:19, 30:23, 38:3-5, 38:24-25; Ex. 2:2, 21:22; Lev. 12:2; Num. 11:12; Judg. 13:2-7; Ruth 4:13; 1 Sam. 1:20, 2:21, 4:19; 2 Sam. 11:5; 2 Kings 8:12, 15:16; 1 Chron. 4:17, 7:23; Job 10:8-12, 31:15; Ps. 51:5, 139:13-15; Ecc. 11:5; Is. 7:14, 8:3, 26:17-18, 44:2, 44:24, 49:5; Jer. 1:4-5, 20:17, 31:8; Hos. 1:3, 1:6, 1:8, 2:5, 12:3, 13:16; Amos 1:13; Matt. 1:18-23; Luke 1:24, 1:31, 1:36

There is no ambiguity in this declaration. In Genesis, we clearly see that when God made man and woman He made them in His image.

> Then God said, "Let us make man in our image, after our likeness. And let them have dominion over the fish of the sea and over the birds of the heavens and over the livestock and over all the earth and over every creeping thing that creeps on the earth." So God created man in his own image, in the image of God he created him; male and female he created them. And God blessed them. And God said to them, "Be fruitful and multiply and fill the earth and subdue it, and have dominion over the fish of the sea and over the birds of the heavens and over every living thing that moves on the earth." (Gen. 2:26-28)

So if mankind is made in the image of God, then at what point does a baby take on that image? Is it after a baby is born? Scripture clearly articulates that from conception a baby is knit together in the womb by God:

> For you formed my inward parts;
>   you knitted me together in my mother's womb.
>   I praise you, for I am fearfully and wonderfully made.
>   Wonderful are your works;
>   my soul knows it very well.
>   My frame was not hidden from you,
>   when I was being made in secret,
>   intricately woven in the depths of the earth.
>   Your eyes saw my unformed substance;
>   in your book were written, every one of them,
>   the days that were formed for me,
>   when as yet there was none of them. (Ps. 139:13-16)

If a baby is a gift, an image bearer of God knit together in his or her mother's womb by God, then the clear inference here is that this baby is a full image bearer from conception.

In case this seems like a bit of a stretch, let me use a few examples of babies being recognized in the womb as preborn persons. Though it did not end well in Genesis with Cain and Abel, we see an example of the Bible recognizing a baby in the womb as a preborn child with the first children born to Adam and Eve:

> Now Adam knew Eve, his wife, and she conceived and bore Cain, saying, "I have gotten a man with the help of the LORD." And again, she bore his brother Abel. Now Abel was a keeper of sheep, and Cain a worker of the ground. (Gen. 4:1-2)

The Son of God was recognized as a preborn baby, not a clump of cells, even in the prophecy of His coming, which was written over 800 years before His birth. This is perhaps the ultimate example of the child in the womb being recognized as an image bearer of God. "Therefore the Lord himself will give you a sign. Behold, the virgin shall conceive and bear a son, and shall call his name Immanuel." (Isa. 7:14)

To conceive not merely potential life but a son is a direct refutation of the argument that life does not begin at conception. Once Jesus was conceived by the Holy Spirit in Mary's womb, He was immediately recognized as a child, not a "potential life." Even preborn baby John in Elizabeth's womb validated the humanity and life of preborn baby Jesus in Mary's womb!

> In those days Mary arose and went with haste into the hill country, to a town in Judah, and she entered the house of Zechariah and greeted Elizabeth. And when Elizabeth heard the greeting of Mary, the baby leaped in her womb. And Elizabeth was filled with the Holy Spirit, and she exclaimed with a loud cry, "Blessed are you among women, and blessed is the fruit of your womb! And why is this granted to me that the mother of my Lord should come to me? For behold, when the sound of your greeting came to my ears, the baby in my womb leaped for joy. And blessed is she who believed

that there would be a fulfillment of what was spoken to her from the Lord." (Luke 1:39-45)

Let's talk a little more technical and scientifically. Jérôme Lejeune M.D., Ph.D., (1924-1994) was a renowned geneticist who received the Kennedy Prize for discovering the gene that causes Down Syndrome. He testified in court in 1989 and presented evidence supporting the biological reality of the preborn child being a unique human person at fertilization. Here are the court transcripts.

Individual Uniqueness

THE WITNESS: We know much more, since the last two years, we know that the uniqueness of the early human being I was talking at the beginning, which was a statistical certainty (but an inference of all we knew about the frequency of the genes, about the difference between individuals) is now an experimentally demonstrated fact. That has been discovered less than two years ago by Jeffreys in England, the remarkable manipulator of DNA. And Jeffreys invented that he could select a little piece of DNA, of which he could manufacture a lot of it, which is specific of some message in our chromosomes. It is repeated a lot of times in many different chromosomes and which is probably a regulation system. Some indication to do something or do another thing, but not a kitchen recipe, but a precision about what to do.

And because it's only telling the cells that this should work and this should not work, it can assume a lot of tiny change, so that there are so many of those little genes and there are so many little changes in them that we receive from father and from mother an array of those genes that we can realize very simply, you get the DNA, you put it in solution and you have it spread in a special medium. Then you put this special probe made by Jeffreys, and what you see it looks exactly like the bar code that you have probably seen in the supermarket, that is, small lines of different breadth and different distance from each other. If you put that bar code and you read it with an electronic device, it tells the computer what the price of the object is and tells a lot of other things.

Well, it's exactly what it tells us that when we look at the DNA bar code, and we detect every individual is different from the next one by its own bar code. And that is not any longer a demonstration by statistical reasoning. So many investigations have been made that we know now that looking at the bar code with his Jeffreys system, the probability that you will find it identical in another person is less than one in a billion. So it's not any longer a theory that each of us in unique. It's now a demonstration as simple as a barcode in the supermarket. It does not tell you the price of human life, it has a difference with supermarket.

The second advance has been that we know now that in one cell we can detect its originality. That has been due to the discovery of a new system which is called PCR, which is becoming extraordinarily popular. It started two years ago. You can take a tiny piece of DNA, one molecule taken from one cell, you see how little this is, you can with that technique reproduce it by billions, and when you have enough you can make the analysis of Jeffreys and see again that we have the whole demonstration of uniqueness, not only in a sample taken from the individual, but in one cell, in one nucleus of one individual.

Another is a third discovery which is by far the most important of all, which is that DNA is not as dull as the magnetic tape I was talking about before. Nature is imitated by our discoveries, but she has known much more than we have yet discovered. In that sense, that the message written on DNA is written by change of the various bases which come one after the other in that one meter long molecule. But now it happens that twenty years ago it was described with certainty that some of the bases of DNA were carrying an extra little piece we call a methyl, (which is CH_3) which is just hooked on it and change a little of the form of one of the bars of this long scale which is the DNA molecule. Nobody understood what it was meaning. And it's only four years ago (especially by the discovery of Surani) that we have begun to understand that we were up to something extraordinary, which is that those tiny little bits of methyl which are put on the base, cytosine, which is transformed in methyl—cytosine—I'm sorry to be technical, your Honor, but I cannot translate it, it's chemical slang.

THE COURT: I understand.

Underscoring Life

...THE WITNESS: Is exactly comparable to what an intelligent reader does when he wants with a pen to underline, to highlight some passage or to scratch, delete another sentence? That is with the methylation, one gene which is still there is knocked out, put to silence, but if it is demethylated on the next division, on the next cell, then it will speak again.

Now, the basic discovery was that this is possible because this tiny change on the DNA, changes the surface of the big groove of the helix of DNA. It is inside this big groove that some molecules, some proteins will hook on different segments specific of the DNA. It is a kind of language telling to the chromosome: You have to tell this information or for this information, shut up, do not speak this one for the moment. It's very necessary, because there is so much information in our cells that if they were expressing everything, every time, to have the energy spent by one cell would be much more than the energy of our whole body. So it's necessary that we have some silent gene and some gene giving expression, expressed.

Now, the basic discovery is the following, and it is directly related to our discussion: That the DNA carried by the sperm is not underlined (or crossed) by this methylation on the same places which are not equivalent in the DNA chromosomes carried by ovum. During the manufacture of the sperm there are indications, it's penciled, so to speak. It's underlined, you should do that. But on the equivalent gene, on the equivalent chromosome manufactured by the mother, the underline is in a different place, and it underlines something different. So that at the moment the two sets of chromosomes carried by the sperms and the egg are put together, they are not as we believed for years identical. We knew there was a difference with the X" and Y" chromosomes, but for the others they were believed to carry the same information; that is not true. Some information is to be read on as coming from the male chromosome, and another information from a chromosome coming from the mother. Now, the reason is that the fertilized egg is the most specialized cell under the sun because it has a special indication underlining segments of DNA which shall be expressed and others that shall not be expressed that no other cell will ever have in the life of this individual. When it's split in two we know that exchange of information comes from one cell to the other one. When it's split in three it receives information we are an individual. And when it continues progressively, the underlining system is progressively changed so that cells do differentiate, and cells become specialized doing a nail, doing hair, doing skin, doing neurons, doing everything.

The Master Program

...And the very thing is that during this process, the expansion of the primary formula which is written in the early human being, nothing is learned but progressively a lot of things are forgotten. The first cell knew more than the three cell stage, and the three cell stage knew more than the morula, than the gastrula, than the primitive streak, and the primitive nervous system. In the beginning it was written really not only what is the genetic message we can read in every cell, but it was written the way it should be read from one sequence to another one. Exactly like in the program of a computer, you don't put only the equivalent of the Algebraic formula, but you tell to the computer do that; if you get that result, then go at that and continue that program; or if you don't get the result, continue and go to the other program. That is written in the first cell; is progressively forgotten in the other cells of our body.

At the end of the process when the organism has grown up, it produce then its own reproductive cells, it puts the counter to zero again, and hence the rejuvenation. A new life will begin when a female and a male cell will encounter to produce the next generation. So I would say very precisely, your Honor, that two years ago I would not have been able to give you this very simple but extremely valuable information which we have now, beyond any doubt.

I would give you an example of why it's not theoretical. We can manipulate with mice—not me, but my colleagues. And with mice they have been able to make pseudo zygote, that is, to take one egg, expel its own legitimate nucleus and put, for example, two nuclei coming from sperm, so they have diploid cell, a diploid zygote containing only two sets of paternal origin; it fails to grow. They have tried to do it with two maternal original nuclei, that is, two maternal chromosomal cells and no paternal cells. It's diploid; by the old theory it should grow, but it does not. But curiously both of them do something; they don't build a full imago, that is, the whole form. But they specialize. If there is only male nuclei, two male nuclei making what is called an androgenote, it produce little cysts which are looking like the membranes and placenta that the child is normally building around himself to make its space and time capsule so that it could take the fluid from the mother vessels. An early zygote containing only male chromosome does only that.

If a zygote contains only chromosomes from female origin, it makes the spare parts. It makes pieces of skin, it makes piece of teeth, it can make a little nail, but all that in a full disorder, not at all constructed it makes the spare parts. We know this directly by experiment in mice done by Surani last year. But we knew that but we could not understood it before.

We knew that already in man, because in man we know that there are what is called dermoid cysts which is a division of a non-fertilized egg inside the ovary of a virgin girl. It cannot grow. It's rare, but it is well known. It will never give a little baby, but it makes the spare parts, teeth, nails, all that mixed in incomprehensible disorder. On the reverse we knew that sometime after apparently normal fertilization the product does not divide correctly but makes cysts, little balls again and again and again, and it's called a mole, hydatidiformis mole, and it's very dangerous because it can give the cancer to the pregnant woman.

Now, we have discovered—(not me), you have to know I'm professor and when I say we, it's all the professors of the world, it's not me. We have discovered that in those hydatidiformis moles, there were only paternal chromosomes. There were two sets of paternal chromosomes and the maternal pronuclei had died, we don't know why. So we know by the mice experiments that it is related to methylation of the DNA.

Hence, we know by the human observation, that there is a specialization of information carried by the sperm compared to the information carried by the ovum. And I would say I was wondering, not surprised, but wondering that we were discovering at this extraordinarily tiny level of information built into the chromosomes, that paternal duty was to build the shelter and to make the gathering of the food, to build the hut and the hunting. And that the maternal trick was household and building of the spare parts so the individual can build himself. And it's a kind of admiration that we have for nature that since we have seen in the grown up that the man is going hunting and the mother is doing the kitchen, it is just the same deeply written inside our own chromosomes at the very beginning at the moments the first human constitution is spelled out.

Well, I have abused your kindness, your Honor. I have spoken maybe too much, but I would say to finish that there is no, no difficulty to understand that at the very beginning of life, the genetic information and the molecular structure of the egg, the spirit and

> the matter, the soul and the body must be that tightly intricated because it's a beginning of the new marvel that we call a human. It's very remarkable for the geneticist that we use the same word to define an idea coming into our mind and a new human coming into life. We use only one word: Conception. We conceive an idea, we conceive a baby. And genetics tell us you are not wrong using the same word; because what is conception? It's really giving information written in the matter so that this matter is now not any longer matter but is a new man.[32]

In simplest terms, the good doctor Jérôme is saying we cannot refute that conception begins at the moment of fertilization; at that moment, everything needed to determine a baby's unique characteristics is present! The rest of what he states is all the bells and whistles to explain the intricacy of the process. What's important to note is that what he states is indisputable in the field of genetics.

The personhood of the preborn baby from fertilization is an incontrovertible biblical and biological fact. Therefore, the biblically consistent logic is simple. Because a child in the womb is a person at fertilization, he or she is a full image bearer of God. Therefore, if the child is a full image bearer of God, then the Christian must argue for equal protection and equal justice from fertilization (biblical conception) for the preborn baby. There is no other biblical alternative.

Now that we have established the fact that the preborn baby is a person and a full image bearer of God, not simply a "potential life," we will move on to explore this concept of equal protection and equal justice for the preborn baby. To recognize that murder is taking place and do nothing about it is a sin, and the blood of the children murdered rests on those who had the opportunity to bring about justice but failed to do so or neglected to. The

---

[32] Servicio Evangélico de Documentación e Información, "What Is in the Fridge? Jerome Lejeune's Expert Court Testimony Regarding the Nature of Human Embryos," www.sedin.org, February 1989, http://www.sedin.org/propeng/embryos.htm.

late Anglican minister, Ezekiel Hopkins, who lived from 1634 to 1690, once said this about negligence and murder culpability:

> Murder is a crying sin. Blood is loud and clamorous. That first [blood] that ever was shed was heard as far as from earth to heaven: "The voice of thy brother's blood crieth unto me from the ground" (Gen 4:10). God will certainly hear its cry and avenge it. But, not only he whose hands are embrued in the blood of others, but those also who are accessory are guilty of murder. As,
>
> (1) Those who command or counsel it to be done. Thus, David became guilty of the murder of innocent Uriah; and God, in drawing up his charge, accuseth him with it: "Thou hast slain him with the sword of the children of Ammon" (2 Sa 12:9).
>
> (2) Those who consent to murder are guilty of it. Thus Pilate, for yielding to the clamorous outcries of the Jews, "Crucify him, Crucify him" (Luke 23:21), though he washed his hands and disavowed the fact, was as much guilty as those who nailed Him to the cross.
>
> (3) He that concealeth a murder is guilty of it. Therefore, we read that in case a man were found slain and the murderer unknown, the elders of that city were to assemble, wash their hands, and protest "Our hands have not shed this blood, neither have our eyes seen it" (Deuteronomy 21:6-7), intimating that if they had seen and concealed it, they had thereby become guilty of the murder.
>
> (4) Those who are in authority and do not punish a murderer, when committed and known, are themselves guilty of it. Thus, when Naboth was condemned to die by the wicked artifice of Jezebel—although Ahab knew nothing of the contrivance until after the execution—yet, because he did not vindicate that innocent blood when he came to the knowledge of it, the prophet chargeth it upon him. "Hast thou killed, and also taken possession?" (1 Kings 21:19). The guilt lay upon him, and the punishment due to it overtook him, although we do not read that he was any otherwise

guilty of it than in not punishing those who had committed it. And those magistrates who, upon any respect whatsoever, suffer a murderer to escape unpunished are said to pollute the land with blood: "Moreover ye shall take no satisfaction for the life of a murderer, which is guilty of death: but he shall be surely put to death...So ye shall not pollute the land wherein ye are: for blood it defileth the land: and the land cannot be cleansed of the blood that is shed therein, but by the blood of him that shed it" (Numbers 35:31, 33).[33]

Strong words spoken by the 15th century Anglican minister, aren't they? Even in the 15th century the standard was that those culpable for the murder of an image bearer of God must bear the justice prescribed by Scripture for murder. It was believed that for a magistrate to neglect this righteous standard of justice was to stain the land with the blood of the innocent person who was murdered. Do we not still believe this? O how red the stain is on our nation! Friends, if the preborn baby is a full image bearer of God from conception, then the baby deserves equal protection and, necessarily, equal justice.

As Christians, we are to recognize that life begins at conception, which happens at fertilization. This language is very important. When talking about when life begins, we must note that an image bearer of God is created at the moment that the sperm of a man combines with the egg of a woman; at that moment, God begins the process of knitting together the body of the child in his or her mother's womb. In short, we call this conception.

Unfortunately, the term "conception" has been under attack, and we have begun to see an unbiblical distinction made in many circles, even "Christian" ones. There is an attempt to call the implantation of a fertilized egg in the mother's uterus "conception." In reality, "conception" happens at the moment of fertilization. This distinction matters because all the elements needed

---

[33] Ezekiel Hopkins, "Thou Shalt Not Kill," in *Abortion* (Pensacola, FL: Chapel Library, 2012), 3–4.

for life to begin in the womb are present when the egg is fertilized by the sperm. Therefore, the beginning life is not dependent upon implantation. It is a scientific fact that at the moment of fertilization all the necessary DNA is present for the development of the child inside and outside the womb.

To argue that conception begins at implantation is foolishness. First, to say that conception begins at implantation dismisses the personhood of the baby that is lost in an ectopic pregnancy. Second, to dismiss that conception happens at fertilization is to dismiss the work that God is doing at the very beginning. What does the word "conceive" mean in this context other than to begin a pregnancy?

Friends, brothers, sisters, conception is not upon implantation. That is a pharmaceutical industry lie designed to deceive Christians into buying contraceptives and to buy into the "family planning" narrative. This deceptive lie was derived from the teachings of Margaret Singer (founder of Planned Parenthood), not from the Bible. The Bible doesn't say we plan a family any more than seeking a life-long spouse to begin one with. Believers, the creation mandate is "be fruitful and multiply," not "plan how many children you will allow God to bless you with."

For those who profess to be Christians who live by God's Word as the supreme standard for their lives, they must affirm what Scripture affirms or find themselves opposing the very words of the living God. Scripture is clear on the idea that image bearers of God are equal in value regardless of what their economic productivity or contribution might be. We clearly see that from the moment of fertilization, all human beings are created equal and have equal value before God because all are made by God in His own image. Just look at what we are told in Proverbs 22:2. "The rich and the poor meet together; the LORD is the Maker of them all."

What this verse is saying is that both rich and poor people are image bearers because they are made in the image of God, not because of their net worth. Please understand that image bearer status is not determined by economic value or perceived contribution to society. For those wondering what other passages talk about this biblical principle of equal value before God, I have included more in the footnotes.[34]

---

[34] Gen. 1:26-27, 5:1, 9:6; James 3:9

8

Defining the Biblical Response

"There is no way to provide equal justice for preborn people without actually giving them the same justice that born people enjoy. Abortion is either illegal, with a sanction attached for anyone who violates, or it's merely moral counsel with no force of law." -Zach Conover[35]

Simply put, the argument is this: The preborn child should have the same rights and protections under the law as any other born person would have from fertilization (natural conception) to natural death. Let me unpack this concept by way of a hypothetical case.

There is a young pregnant woman who is excited about her pregnancy. One day, she stops at a gas station and goes in to use the restroom. A man armed with a gun comes into the gas station intending to rob the store. A noble bystander engages the man with the gun in an altercation. The young pregnant woman comes out of the restroom and sees the scuffle between the two men over the gun. She freezes in fear and, in the scuffle, the gun goes off and the bullet hits her. The scuffle ends and the robber runs out the door but is caught soon after. Tragically, the woman and her preborn baby die from

---

[35] Zachary Conover, "There Is No Way to Provide Equal Justice for Preborn People...," www.twitter.com, September 5, 2023, https://twitter.com/ZacharyConover/status/1699127452264742941?s=20.

the gunshot wound. In court, the Christian prosecutor desires to pursue the full extent of the law's judgment on the man who brought the gun in to rob the store by accusing him of one count of armed robbery and two counts of manslaughter.

Why is the prosecutor pursuing two counts of manslaughter? Is the prosecutor acting righteously or naively and emotionally? I am here to argue that the prosecutor is a righteous prosecutor who rightly understands God's law. By pursuing two counts of manslaughter, the prosecutor is treating the preborn baby as a living person and establishing a precedent of equal justice.

Now you may be thinking, "Well, that's a made up story, Mike!"

Not so fast. There are countless stories of pregnant women being killed, whether by accident or murdered, and in some cases they are murdered for their preborn babies. One such story is so heinous I will only give the immediate details and footnote a link to the whole story. The story is stomach-turning because two image bearers were ruthlessly murdered.

There was a woman in Texas who intentionally befriended a woman who was 34 weeks pregnant. This woman intended to rip the baby from her womb and pretend the baby was hers because she had had a hysterectomy and could no longer have children for her boyfriend. She ruthlessly murdered the pregnant woman and cut the baby from the womb who later died as a result of the trauma. The woman was found driving around with the dead baby in her lap and the mother of the child was found dead with a huge laceration to her belly from hip to hip.[36]

According to a report by CNN, the jury made their decision on guilt after only an hour of deliberation. CNN said,

> A Texas woman convicted of killing a pregnant woman and then taking her unborn baby, who also died, has been sentenced to death, court records show. A Bowie County jury last month after about

---

[36] Leonardo Blair, "'Evil Piece of Flesh Demon:' Woman Sentenced to Death for Killing Pregnant Friend to Steal Unborn Baby," The Christian Post, November 11, 2022, https://www.christianpost.com/news/texas-woman-sentenced-to-death-for-murdering-pregnant-friend.html.

an hour of deliberations found Taylor Rene Parker guilty of capital murder in the deaths of Reagan Michelle Simmons and her baby, the district attorney's office previously said. The same jury was then tasked with choosing her sentence – death or prison without parole. The jury handed down the death sentence Wednesday, online court records show.[37]

Did this rush to judgment align with God's standard of judgment for murder? Due process considered, it seems to have come in alignment. They weighed all the factors that played into the motive for the murder.
Would we not ask for the same process to be used in prosecuting a murderer of a 2-year-old? Why then do we not ask for this process to take place with the murder of preborn children? For crying out loud, CNN, a liberal news network who has been on record often promoting abortion rights, accurately reports on this case. They even refer to the preborn child as a baby rather than a fetus. Why the inconsistency? Why does it take such heinous circumstances for us to see the need for justice to be served?

It ultimately boils down to a worldview issue. Who is it that defines the standard rule of law as it pertains to murder? Of course, as a Christian, I argue that God's Word defines the standard.

Any act of preborn homicide is murder and is deserving of criminal prosecution, regardless of how much press it receives. Since abortion unjustly destroys an image bearer of God, should not our reaction be the same? Just as your stomach turned reading about the murder of Reagan Michelle Simmons and her preborn baby, your stomach too must turn with the ever increasing number of preborn children ruthlessly murdered in their mothers' wombs by pill, suction, or surgical abortion.

Let us look at God's standard and see what God has to say about our hypothetical case from the beginning of this chapter:

---

[37] Rebekah Riess, "A Texas Woman Found Guilty of Killing a Pregnant Woman to Take Her Unborn Child Has Been Sentenced to Death," CNN, November 10, 2022, https://www.cnn.com/2022/11/10/us/texas-pregnant-woman-killed-death-sentence/index.html.

"When men strive together and hit a pregnant woman, so that her children come out, but there is no harm, the one who hit her shall surely be fined, as the woman's husband shall impose on him, and he shall pay as the judges determine. But if there is harm, then you shall pay life for life, eye for eye, tooth for tooth, hand for hand, foot for foot, burn for burn, wound for wound, stripe for stripe." (Ex. 21:22-25)

This law found in Exodus concerns a hypothetical very similar to ours. When two men are fighting and accidentally wound a pregnant woman, the one who harms the pregnant woman or her baby is guilty. If the baby is born with no harm, then the offender is to be fined at the husband's choosing. However, if the baby and/or woman is harmed or killed, the biblical warrant is clear: "you shall pay life for life, eye for eye, tooth for tooth, hand for hand, foot for foot, burn for burn, wound for wound, stripe for stripe." (Ex. 21:23b-25)

It is abundantly evident here that the prosecutor in our hypothetical case at the beginning of this chapter is acting justly according to God's law. God's standard of justice does not differentiate between the baby in the womb and the born person when it comes to the value of his/her life. However, it is a tragic reality that there are many cases in which mankind has chosen to weigh situations unjustly out of emotionally-driven, arbitrary distinctions. In doing so, man has deprived the preborn image bearer of God true justice.

An Example of Unjust Legislation

Let's look at the laws on the books in the state of Ohio as it relates to the murder of the preborn baby:

> A. No person shall purposely cause the death of another or the unlawful termination of another's pregnancy.
> B. No person shall cause the death of another as a proximate result of the offender's committing or attempting to commit an offense of violence that is a felony of the first or second degree and

that is not a violation of section 2903.03 or 2903.04 of the Revised Code.

C. Division (B) of this section does not apply to an offense that becomes a felony of the first or second degree only if the offender previously has been convicted of that offense or another specified offense.

D. Whoever violates this section is guilty of murder, and shall be punished as provided in section 2929.02 of the Revised Code.[38]

However, in the criminal code we have an example of hypocrisy and double standard by withholding justice from the preborn baby. The law stipulates that the baby ruthlessly murdered in the case of voluntary abortion deserves no justice because the mother volunteered their murder; the mother is not culpable, regardless of motive or malice aforethought, and no reason need be mentioned. Here is a portion of the convoluted and intentionally morally foggy code:[39]

A. "Unlawful termination of another's pregnancy" means causing the death of an unborn member of the species homo sapiens, who is or was carried in the womb of another, as a result of injuries inflicted during the period that begins with fertilization and that continues unless and until live birth occurs.

B. "Another's unborn" or "such other person's unborn" means a member of the species homo sapiens, who is or was carried in the womb of another, during a period that begins with fertilization and that continues unless and until live birth occurs.

Sounds good so far, but here is the sleight of hand and what makes these laws

---

[38] Ohio Legislative Service Commission, "Ohio Revised Code Section 2903.02: Murder," June 30, 1998, https://codes.ohio.gov/ohio-revised-code/section-2903.02

[39] Ohio Legislative Service Commission, "Ohio Revised Code Section 2903.09: Unlawful Termination of Another's Pregnancy," March 22, 2019, https://codes.ohio.gov/ohio-revised-code/section-2903.09

now unjust:

> C. Notwithstanding divisions (A) and (B) of this section, in no case shall the definitions of the terms "unlawful termination of another's pregnancy," "another's unborn," and "such other person's unborn" that are set forth in division (A) of this section be applied or construed in any of the following manners:
>
> (1) Except as otherwise provided in division (C)(1) of this section, **in a manner so that the offense prohibits or is construed as prohibiting any pregnant woman or her physician from performing an abortion with the actual consent of the pregnant woman, with the consent of the pregnant woman implied by law in a medical emergency, or with the approval of one otherwise authorized by law to consent to medical treatment on behalf of the pregnant woman.** An abortion that violates the conditions described in the immediately preceding sentence may be punished as a violation of section 2903.01, 2903.02, 2903.03, 2903.04, 2903.05, 2903.06, 2903.08, 2903.11, 2903.12, 2903.13, 2903.14, 2903.21, or 2903.22 of the Revised Code, as applicable. An abortion that does not violate the conditions described in the second immediately preceding sentence, but that does violate section 2919.12, division (B) of section 2919.13, or section 2919.15, 2919.151, 2919.17, or 2919.18 of the Revised Code, may be punished as a violation of section 2919.12, division (B) of section 2919.13, or section 2919.15, 2919.151, 2919.17, or 2919.18 of the Revised Code, as applicable. (emphasis added)

Did you catch what was written before all the worthless pro-life restrictions? A law that is meant to protect human life promotes the destruction of it! This law also allows the woman who willfully pays the hitman to commit prenatal homicide (we call them abortionists, but let's be honest here, that just means paid assassin) or commits the atrocious offense herself walks away with legal impunity. This stipulation/loophole (whatever you desire to refer to it as) is in every state law "restricting" abortion. In all actuality, it keeps abortion legal in all 50 states. Continue with me:

2. In a manner so that the offense is applied or is construed as applying to a woman based on an act or omission of the woman that occurs while she is or was pregnant and that results in any of the following:
(a) Her delivery of a stillborn baby;
(b) Her causing, in any other manner, the death in utero of an unborn that she is carrying;
(c) Her causing the death of her child who is born alive but who dies from one or more injuries that are sustained while the child is an unborn;
(d) Her causing her child who is born alive to sustain one or more injuries while the child is an unborn;
(e) Her causing, threatening to cause, or attempting to cause, in any other manner, an injury, illness, or other physiological impairment, regardless of its duration or gravity, or a mental illness or condition, regardless of its duration or gravity, to an unborn that she is carrying.

Hard to read, isn't it?

The aforementioned stipulation conflates abortion (the willful taking of a preborn life) with delivering a stillborn baby (an already dead baby). It shows very little concern for medical accuracy and is wholly inappropriate language to be included in a law talking about abortion, because stillbirth medical procedures are fundamentally and medically not called abortions.

Unjust laws teach people injustice and propagate deception. It's infuriating to recognize that we have not been discipling nor holding legislators accountable on their God-given duties to write just legislation that honors God. We must challenge them to avoid promoting godlessness in any fashion. Compromises like this type of legal language lead to the mass murdering of millions of our preborn neighbors and it must be stopped. To legislate with partiality toward the mother of the murdered preborn is an abomination before God according to His Word.

In the year 2023, all laws across our country make the same exceptions for abortion in one form or another. As if this is not bad enough, bills proposed by professing "Christian" legislators make these same exceptions, which allow abortion to continue.

It is now also the case that as of November 2023, Ohio allows abortion up until birth by using the following language on a state constitutional amendment:

> A. Every individual has a right to make and carry out one's own reproductive decisions, including but not limited to decisions on:
> 1. contraception;
> 2. fertility treatment;
> 3. continuing one's own pregnancy;
> 4. miscarriage care; and
> 5. abortion.
>
> B. The State shall not, directly or indirectly, burden, penalize, prohibit, interfere with, or discriminate against either:
> 1. An individual's voluntary exercise of this right or
> 2. A person or entity that assists an individual exercising this right, unless the State demonstrates that it is using the least restrictive means to advance the individual's health in accordance with widely accepted and evidence-based standards of care. However, abortion may be prohibited after fetal viability. But in no case may such an abortion be prohibited if in the professional judgment of the pregnant patient's treating physician it is necessary to protect the pregnant patient's life or health.
>
> C. As used in this Section:
> 1. "Fetal viability" means "the point in a pregnancy when, in the professional judgment of the pregnant patient's treating physician, the fetus has a significant likelihood of survival outside the uterus with reasonable measures. This is determined on a case-by-case

basis."

    2. "State" includes any governmental entity and any political subdivision.

    D. This Section is self-executing.[40]

As a Christian, when I read legislation that is so devoid of righteousness I get angry that biblically principled Christians have stepped out of the public sphere and have handed it over to politically motivated "Christians" and secular humanists; neither have a concept on how to build laws or write just legislation. The first group doesn't read the Bible very often, or at all, nor do they have a true relationship with Christ as Lord. The other group outright rejects God and seeks to undo God-honoring legislation. Honestly, both are equally considered children of the devil; one group is dressed Republican and boasts "conservative" titles while the other group plays its cards right on the table as flamingly liberal. When the two go to battle in the House or the Senate, the unprincipled Republicans move ever closer to liberalism. Even when they win on legislation, the win is a farce. It is so because their sense of morality is not adjusted to God's standards of justice!

    John Calvin once said this about murder,

> To be clear of the crime of murder, it is not enough to refrain from shedding man's blood. If in act you perpetrate, if in endeavor you plot, if in wish and design you conceive what is adverse to another's safety, you have the guilt of murder. On the other hand, if you do not according to your means and opportunity study to defend his safety, by that inhumanity you violate the law.[41]

O Christian, we live in a society plagued by many distortions of what true

---

[40] State of Ohio, "The Right to Reproductive Freedom with Protections for Health and Safety," Article 1, Section 22 § (2023), https://codes.ohio.gov/ohio-constitution/section-1.22.

[41] John Calvin, "Sixth Commandment, Institutes of the Christian Religion Book 2," biblestudytools.com, 1845, https://www.biblestudytools.com/history/calvin-institutes-christianity/book2/chapter-8/sixth-commandment.html.

justice is, and we as the church should not be silent during these times. We stand on the shoulders of giants who laid their lives down so that we would be able to have the faith we have. Let us also be willing to lay our lives down for the preborn child.

Real Justice is Derived From the Bible

Now that we have talked about compromised legislators and unbiblical legislation, let's talk about real justice. I mention once again that the perfect example of justice is found in the Gospel of Jesus Christ. To distort God's standard of equal justice is to inevitably distort a right understanding of the Gospel. Look with me one more time at this beautiful yet tragically necessary picture of justice. It is through the righteous wrath of God being poured out on Jesus Christ that cosmic justice is had. (2 Cor. 5:21)

Let that sink in. In fact, let me be a little more direct.

The ruthless, premeditated murder of the Son of God demonstrates God's righteousness and perfect love. You may be thinking, "How on earth is the injustice of Jesus on the cross, the only perfect man, being wrongfully accused and crucified the best example of true justice?" (Rom. 5:17-21)

Friend, though Jesus was innocent and wrongfully maligned, He voluntarily went to the cross. He became the sin bearer for us so that those of us who repent of our sins and confess Jesus as Lord might be given His righteousness. This act of substitution on our behalf made Him guilty in our stead; He received the just wrath of God for our sins. Therefore, we see God's infinitely just judgment poured out on His perfect Son in the substitutionary atonement because God's perfect plan of redemption was that Jesus would be our righteous substitute. In short, the punishment meant for us was poured out on Jesus. This is justice because only perfect blood was acceptable to be shed for the remission of sins. (Rom. 8:32-39)

So what does this justice look like today? If we are truly operating with equal standards of justice, then we should be treating the murderer as a murderer and the thief as a thief, not victims of circumstance. The argument that the mother who murders her baby is always a victim and should never be punished for it, simply put, doesn't work with any other crime. For instance, we would never say that a pedophile is a victim of circumstance and therefore should never be punished; no, just laws require punishment and culpability for those that break them. Our past experiences or good deeds weigh little in how we should be punished. The murderer is not punished less because he once was a "straight-A" student or helped an old lady cross the street. No, he is punished for the crime he committed. His upbringing may be studied as a causal factor, but he must own his moral decision to murder and all the consequences that come with that action.

Likewise, though an abortionist is a special kind of evil person, we know that no abortionist walks the streets seeking pregnant women to attack. We also know the preborn baby in the womb of its mother is a full image bearer of God from fertilization. Additionally, we know that God's standard of justice requires that we provide the same protections to that preborn baby that we would provide for any other born person. So this necessarily means what?

We must rightly conclude this legally and morally profound application of equal protection and equal justice to mean that we equally apply the laws on protecting against homicide to the preborn person as we would to any other born person. The argument and stipulation is wholly biblical; it is commanded in Scripture as our only response to murder.

A Real World Example Of Righteous Legislation

I will conclude this chapter by sharing an example of righteous legislation that could be presented to a legislator in your state:

> Be it enacted by the General Assembly of the State of _____:
> SECTION 1. Purpose.
> Acknowledging the sanctity of innocent human life, created in the image of God, which should be equally protected from the beginning of biological development to natural death, the purpose of this act is:

(A) To fully recognize the personhood of a living human preborn child from the beginning of biological development at the moment of fertilization upon the fusion of a human spermatozoon with a human ovum.

(B) To ensure the right to life and equal protection of the laws to all preborn children by protecting them with the same homicide laws protecting all other human persons.

(C) To recognize that the Constitution of the United States, and the laws of the United States which shall be made in pursuance thereof, are the supreme law of the land and they irrefutably declare that all persons have the right to life.

(D) To treat as void and of no effect any and all federal statutes, regulations, treaties, orders, and court rulings which would deprive a preborn child of the right to life or prohibit the equal protection of such right under the law; and

(E) Therefore, to entirely abolish abortion in this state.

SECTION 2. That section _____ of the Revised Code be enacted to read as follows: _____.

(A) This section may be cited as the "Abolition of Abortion in _____ Act."

(B) Notwithstanding section _____ or any other provision of law, in this chapter.

The terms "person" or "another" shall include a living human child before birth from the beginning of biological development at the moment of fertilization upon the fusion of a human spermatozoon with a human ovum.

(C) Enforcement pursuant to the "Abolition of Abortion in _____ Act" is subject to the same presumptions, defenses, justifications, immunities, and clemencies as would apply to the homicide or assault of a human being who had been born alive.

(a) Any federal statute, regulation, treaty, executive order, or court ruling that purports to supersede, stay, or overrule this section is in violation of the constitution of this state and the Constitution of the United States of America and is therefore void.

(b) This state, any political subdivision of this state, and any agent of this state or a political subdivision of this state that may disregard or defy any part or the whole of any federal court decision which purports to enjoin or void any provision of this section.

(D) Pursuant to the powers granted to the General Assembly by Article _____, sections _____Constitution, any judge of this state who purports to enjoin, stay, overrule, or void any provision of this section shall be subject to impeachment or removal.

(E) This section is prospective only and shall not apply to crimes committed prior to the effective date of this act. For purposes of this section, a crime is committed before the effective date of this act if any element of the crime occurs before the effective date.

(F) The provisions of this section are non severable.

SECTION 3. Necessary Clarifications

(A) A Salpingostomy and Salpingectomy are both separate life-saving medical procedures and are not considered an elective surgical, chemical, or suction abortion. They are done in a qualified and rated medical center not an abortion clinic, to treat the tragedy of ectopic pregnancies.

(a) This act in no way prevents laparoscopic, life-saving, emergency medical treatments that do not intentionally end the life of a living baby. This does not prevent premature birth that may result in the death of the child.

(b) Ectopic pregnancies, miscarriages, or stillbirths are not dealt with by elective surgical abortions, suction abortions or chemical abortions. Therefore, they will not be considered as violations of this act.

SECTION 4. The enactment of Sections 2 of this act is hereby declared to be an emergency measure necessary for the immediate preservation of the public peace, health, and safety.

(A) The reason for such necessity is that an average _____

preborn children are killed via abortion in this state every day. Therefore, the enactment of Section 3 of this act shall go into immediate effect.

The contrast of legislation efforts couldn't be more clear. One compromises God's holy standard of justice, and the other (my sample bill) upholds God's righteous standard of justice for the preborn baby.

9

We Stand With a Great Cloud of Witnesses

"The only thing necessary for the triumph of evil is for good men to do nothing."
-Unknown[42]

Let us begin by reading a helpful summary of abortion and the practices in antiquity written by George Grant. We cannot understand an atrocity so ancient unless we are willing to look at the mess it has made and the stain it has left throughout the ages.

> Virtually every culture in antiquity was stained with the blood of innocent children. Unwanted infants in ancient Rome were abandoned outside the city walls to die from exposure to the elements or from the attacks of wild foraging beasts. Greeks often gave their pregnant women harsh doses of herbal or medicinal abortifacients. Persians developed highly sophisticated surgical curette procedures. Chinese women tied heavy ropes around their waists so excruciatingly tight that they either aborted or passed into

---

[42] The quote is attributed to Irish philosopher Edmund Burke, though there is no evidence that Burke said or wrote these words. The true author remains unknown.

unconsciousness. Ancient Hindus and Arabs concocted chemical pessaries-abortifacients that were pushed or pumped directly into the womb through the birth canal. Primitive Canaanites threw their children onto great flaming pyres as a sacrifice to their god Molech. Polynesians subjected their pregnant women to onerous tortures-their abdomens beaten with large stones or hot coals heaped upon their bodies. Japanese women straddled boiling cauldrons of parricidal brews. Egyptians disposed of their unwanted children by disemboweling and dismembering them shortly after birth-their collagen was then ritually harvested for the manufacture of cosmetic creams. None of the great minds of the ancient world-from Plato and Aristotle to Seneca and Quintilian, from Pythagoras and Aristophanes to Livy and Cicero, from Herodotus and Thucydides to Plutarch and Euripides-disparaged child-killing in any way. In fact, most of them actually recommended it. They callously discussed its various methods and procedures. They casually debated its sundry legal ramifications. They blithely tossed lives like dice. Abortion, infanticide, exposure, and abandonment were so much a part of human societies that they provided the primary "liet motif" (meaning the dominant theme) in popular traditions, stories, myths, fables, and legends.

The founding of Rome was, for instance, presumed to be the happy result of the abandonment of children. According to the story, a vestal virgin who had been raped bore twin sons, Romulus and Remus. The harsh Etruscan monarch Amulius ordered them exposed on the Tiber River. Left in a basket which floated ashore, they were found by a she-wolf and suckled by her. Later, a shepherd discovered them and took them home to his wife, and the kindly couple brought them up as their own. Romulus and Remus would later establish the city of Rome on the seven hills near the place of their rescue.

Oedipus was presumed to be an abandoned child who was also found by a shepherd and later rose to greatness. Ion, the eponymous monarch in ancient Greece miraculously lived through an abortion, according to tradition. Cyrus, the founder of the Persian empire, was supposedly a fortunate survivor of infanticide. According to Homer's legend, Paris, whose amorous indiscretions started the Trojan War, was also a victim of abandonment. Telephus, the king of Mysia in Greece, and Habius, ruler of the Cunetes in Spain, had both been exposed as children according to various folk tales. Jupiter, chief god of the Olympian pantheon, himself had been abandoned as a child. He in turn exposed his twin sons, Zethus and Amphion. Similarly, other myths related that Poseidon, Aesculapius, Hephaistos, Attis, and Cybele had all been abandoned to die.

Because they had been mired by the minions of sin and death, it was as natural as the spring rains for the men and women of antiquity to kill their children. It was as instinctive as the autumn harvest for them to summarily sabotage their own heritage. They saw nothing particularly cruel about despoiling the fruit of their wombs. It was woven into the very fabric of their culture. They believed that it was completely justifiable. They believed that it was just and good and right. But they were wrong. Dreadfully wrong.[43]

Sadly, it is clear that the practices of abortion and child sacrifice have been observed and celebrated by pagan cultures for thousands of years. However, true followers of Christ have been opposed to abortion and child sacrifice since the beginning of the church. The church has been in conflict with this cultural giant for thousands of years, but we have not always faced the giant biblically. In fact, I will petition that the Christian response was only compromised within the last century. The confusion and compromise have been confounded by decades of unbiblical teaching on when life begins and the identity of the baby in the womb.

---

[43] George Grant, *Third Time Around: A History of the Pro-Life Movement from the First Century to the Present* (Brentwood, TN: Wolgemuth & Hyatt, Publishers, Inc., 1991), 12–13.

THE CHRISTIAN RESPONSE TO ABORTION

To prove that the church throughout the ages has been consistent on the biblical response to abortion, here are some quotes from early antiquity and the early church demonstrating that equal justice and equal protection was the irrefutably prominent position for the Christians within the first 400 years of the church.

The early Jewish historian, Josephus, explains the general consensus on abortion during his time. Though not a Christian, in many cases he was a good reflection of the prevailing cultural position.

> The law, moreover, enjoins us to bring up all our offspring and forbids women to cause abortion of what is begotten, or to destroy it afterward; and if any woman appears to have so done, she will be a murderer of her child, by destroying a living creature, and diminishing humankind...[44]

An early church set of teachings known as the Didache, which likely dates back to A.D. 70, says this about abortion:

> The second commandment of the teaching: You shall not murder. You shall not commit adultery. You shall not seduce boys. You shall not commit fornication. You shall not steal. You shall not practice magic. You shall not use potions. You shall not procure [an] abortion, nor destroy a newborn child.[45]

To clarify this teaching further, R. Scott Clark, a writer for the Heidelblog, makes this helpful observation and comment about the Didache's teaching on abortion:

---

[44] Josephus, "Section 25," in *Against Apion: Book 2*, n.d., https://www.biblestudytools.com/history/flavius-josephus/against-apion/book-2/chapter-1.html.

[45] Church Fathers, "The Didache on Abortion," 70AD, https://www.churchfathers.org/abortion.

Yesterday, in class, as we worked through chapter 2 I was struck by this portion of 2:2: "You shall not murder a child in destruction nor shall you kill one just born" (οὐ φονεύσεις τέκνον ἐν φθορᾷ οὐδὲ γεννηθέντα ἀποκτενεῖς). Michael Holmes, in his excellent edition of the Apostolic Fathers (3rd edition) translates these clauses, "you shall not abort a child or commit infanticide." This seems perfect. Lately, however, I've been comparing that edition with the revised Loeb edition of the Apostolic Fathers translated by Bart Ehrman (A secular New Testament scholar who is Agnostic seeking to disprove the Bible), who translates the same clauses, "do not abort a fetus or kill a child that is born." I was struck by Ehrman's choice of fetus, which is Latin for "unborn infant" or "unborn child" instead of "child." Holmes and Ehrman agree that the Didache intends to forbid abortion. The contrast between the "τέκνον (child) in destruction" with that one that has been brought to delivery (γεννηθέντα) seems clear enough. This passage should give pause to those self-identified Christians who glibly announce that they are pro-choice. The Didache was not indifferent about abortion nor does it hesitate to list abortion (and infanticide) with other gross violations of the natural and moral law: murder, adultery, pederasty, sexual immorality, magic and sorcery, coveting, perjury, greed, and conspiracies (2:1–7). The pagans were known to try to induce abortions, which the Didache prohibits. It is hard to imagine the author of the Didache announcing that he is personally opposed to abortion but supported it as a matter of public policy any more than they would say the same about murder of adults, pederasty, and the like.[46]

Athenagoras was a second century early church apologist who is known for

---

[46] R. Scott Clark, "Notes from the Didache on the Early Christian View of Abortion," The Heidelblog, October 7, 2016, https://heidelblog.net/2016/10/notes-from-the-didache-on-the-early-christian-view-of-abortion/.

authoring a defense of the Christian faith to the Emperor Marcus Aurelias and his son, Commodus, in a letter called "The Embassy for the Christians." This letter is one of the earliest examples from the early church demonstrating their acceptance of the concept of the Trinity. Athenagoras had this to say about abortion:

> What man of sound mind, therefore, will affirm, while such is our character, that we are murderers?...When we say that those women who use drugs to bring on abortion commit murder, and will have to give an account to God for the abortion, on what principle should we commit murder? For it does not belong to the same person to regard the very fetus in the womb as a created being, and therefore an object of God's care, and when it has passed into life, to kill it; and not to expose an infant, because those who expose them are chargeable with child-murder, and on the other hand, when it has been reared to destroy it.[47]

The early church father, Tertullian (155-220 A.D), even spoke out against the atrocity of abortion. He made the following statement, which unequivocally condemns the practice of preborn child murder:

> In our case, a murder being once for all forbidden, we may not destroy even the fetus in the womb, while as yet the human being derives blood from the other parts of the body for its sustenance. To hinder a birth is merely a speedier man-killing; nor does it matter whether you take away a life that is born, or destroy one that is coming to birth.[48]

A non-canonical, early Christian text from 130 A.D. titled "The Epistle of

---

[47] Church Fathers, "Athenagoras on Abortion," 177AD, https://www.churchfathers.org/abortion.

[48] Church Fathers, "Turtullian on Abortion," 197AD, https://www.churchfathers.org/abortion.

Barnabas" says this about abortion and infanticide:

> Thou shalt love thy neighbor more than thine own soul. Thou shalt not murder a child by abortion, nor again shalt thou kill it when it is born. Thou shalt not withhold thy hand from thy son or daughter, but from their youth thou shalt teach them the fear of God.[49]

A second to third century theologian named Hippolytus, who was alive from 170 A.D. to 235 A.D., made this declaration about abortion during his day:

> Women who were reputed to be believers began to take drugs to render themselves sterile, and to bind themselves tightly so as to expel what was being conceived, since they would not, on account of relatives and excess wealth, want to have a child by a slave or by any insignificant person. See, then, into what great impiety that lawless one has proceeded, by teaching adultery and murder at the same time![50]

The former Archbishop of Constantinople, John Chrysostom, lived from 347 to 407 A.D. He saw abortion as evil and declared it to be the outpouring fruit of harlotry in a sermon on Romans:

> Wherefore I beseech you, flee fornication....Why sow where the ground makes it its care to destroy the fruit?—where there are many efforts at abortion?—where there is murder before the birth? For even the harlot you do not let continue a mere harlot, but make her a murderess also. You see how drunkenness leads to prostitution, prostitution to adultery, adultery to murder; or rather to something

---

[49] J.B. Lightfoot, "The Epistle of Barnabas (Barnabas 19:5)," www.earlychristianwritings.com, 130AD, https://www.earlychristianwritings.com/text/barnabas-lightfoot.html.

[50] Church Fathers, "Hippolytus on Abortion," 228AD, https://www.churchfathers.org/abortion.

even worse than murder. For I have no name to give it, since it does not take off the thing born, but prevents its being born. Why then do thou abuse the gift of God, and fight with his laws, and follow after what is a curse as if a blessing, and make the chamber of procreation a chamber for murder, and arm the woman that was given for childbearing unto slaughter? For with a view to drawing more money by being agreeable and an object of longing to her lovers, even this she is not backward to do, so heaping upon thy head a great pile of fire. For even if the daring deed be hers, yet the causing of it is thine.[51]

We are told by George Grant that in 330-379 A.D., Basil of Caesarea took several deliberative steps to defend the preborn and those unwanted by their parents, but he was not at all a lone wolf in the Apostolic era:

> Basil was not alone in his affirmation of the Biblical message of life or in his condemnation of child-killing. In fact, the wholehearted consensus of the Apostolic Era was that all life was a sacred gift from God and that any breach of that gift was nothing less than murder. There were no ifs, ands, or buts about it. On that, all of the patristics absolutely agreed.[52]

---

[51] Church Fathers, "John Chrysostom on Abortion," 391AD, https://www.churchfathers.org/abortion.

[52] George Grant, *Third Time Around: A History of the Pro-Life Movement from the First Century to the Present* (Brentwood, TN: Wolgemuth & Hyatt, Publishers, Inc., 1991), 23–24.

A Holocaust is Happening by Permission of the Modern-Day Church…But That Can Change

The early church was clear on how to respond to abortion; unfortunately, we have been anything but clear in the last 100 years. However, we can change that because God's Word gives us undeniable clarity. Fundamentally, Scripture tells us that to not obey the commands of Christ is to be a liar who does not truly abide in Christ. (1 John 2:1-6) Therefore, if we are following God's holy standard of justice, we must truly desire to see abortion ended immediately without exceptions or compromises. Believer, please let your conscience be thoroughly guided by biblical principles. Look at the great cloud of Christian testimony throughout church history.

We have enough people meaning well, but they are causing a mess of things in this fight because they've surrendered to a "what might or might not work" pragmatic approach. I urge you to be biblically-driven and principled in your approach to end abortion. Join the litany of examples throughout church history calling for equal protection and equal justice for the preborn.

As you continue to see how the Christian is supposed to respond to the holocaust of abortion happening all over the world, you will lose sleep, your heart will be burdened, righteous anger and indignation will well up in you, and then you will have to decide how you will respond. You will have to size up the task and discern where you will stand. However, to stay silent must never be an option. To stay silent and do nothing is most assuredly conceding defeat and allowing innocent blood to be shed. It is putting the blood of the innocent on your hands. In Proverbs there is a pertinent passage we must look at as we talk about this need for immediate biblical justice:

> If you faint in the day of adversity, your strength is small. Rescue those who are being taken away to death; hold back those who are stumbling to the slaughter. If you say, "Behold, we did not know this," does not he who weighs the heart perceive it? Does not he who keeps watch over your soul know it, and will he not repay man

according to his work? (Prov. 24:10-12)

May it be that after reading this book you are steeled with courage and biblical warrant for immediate, faithful obedience on how to engage abortion in our land. For we are told that those who truly claim to be followers of Christ and love Jesus will be those who obey His commands. God has not stuttered on His standards of justice; neither has the early church, and neither should we. Let us boldly look to abolish the legal, unjustified slaughter of preborn children in our land by following how God has laid it out for us.

10

What About Exceptions for the Life of the Mother?

Have you ever heard that question? If you haven't, you will. This is the primary question given by the woefully ignorant, well-meaning Christians when they attempt to put their two cents into the ongoing public debate surrounding abortion. This question is the primary objection to legislation that would actually abolish abortion once and for all.

Chances are you know someone or have yourself experienced the tragedy of an ectopic pregnancy. It is in deep sorrow and compassion for those who experience this tragedy that this chapter is written. Though I have compassion on this tragedy, we must not let emotions misguide the facts.

There is a lot of misinformation, even from pastors, on ectopic pregnancies. Ectopic pregnancies are not typically abortions and are more akin to miscarriages than they are to elective surgical, suction, or chemical abortions. Southern Baptists for Abolishing Abortion wrote a great article addressing some of the misinformation on ectopic pregnancies. Here is how they introduce the issue:

> There are rare times in a pregnancy when the child is growing in the mother's body somewhere other than the womb, for example, in the fallopian tube, abdominal cavity, and very rarely inside one

of her ovaries. Typically, doctors consider these pregnancies fatal so abortion is the prescribed solution. "It's better to save the mother by aborting the unborn child than to do nothing and allow both of them to die," they say. Studies show that not all, not even most, ectopic pregnancies threaten the life of the mother.[53]

Procedures dealing with ectopic or extrauterine pregnancies are done in a hospital and not an abortion clinic, because these procedures require real doctors who have the capability to serve both mother and baby. It is considered a rescue operation whereby the doctor attempts, in every way possible, to treat both baby and mother. True doctors understand they have two patients in the case of an ectopic pregnancy. Here are the most common ethically accepted means for doctors to treat extrauterine pregnancies in the United States:

Careful Watching and Waiting

The doctor supervises the mother's condition but waits to see if the baby will implant in the correct location on his/her own or if surgery is going to be needed.[54]

Surgical

The surgical procedures typically used to treat ectopic pregnancies are laparoscopic. This means that two to four small incisions are made in the abdominal and/or pelvic areas in order to perform minimally invasive procedures. One incision is for a laparoscope, which is a small camera used to

---

[53] Dusty Deevers, "What about Ectopic Pregnancies?," Southern Baptists for Abolishing Abortion, June 10, 2020, https://southernbaptistsabolishingabortion.com/2020/06/10/what-about-ectopic-pregnancies/.

[54] End Abortion Now, "Answering the Ectopic Pregnancy Argument," End Abortion Now, March 1, 2023, https://endabortionnow.com/answering-the-ectopic-pregnancy-argument/.

see inside the body, and the other incisions are for the surgical instruments.[55] In the case of an ectopic pregnancy, a doctor will perform a salpingostomy or a salpingectomy.

In these procedures, a small incision is made in the abdomen, near or in the navel. Next, a doctor uses a laparoscope to view the tubal area. In a salpingostomy, the preborn baby is removed and the fallopian tube is left to heal on its own. In a salpingectomy, the preborn baby and the fallopian tube are both removed.[56] Which procedure a woman has depends on the amount of bleeding and damage, and whether or not the tube has ruptured. It is vitally important to note that even before most ectopic pregnancies are detected, the preborn baby has already died. Therefore, these surgical procedures are not abortive in nature.

The Unbiblical and Unnecessary "Life of the Mother" Exception

So many people have a misguided understanding of ectopic pregnancies and the procedures that are most commonly done to treat a woman who has a baby developing ectopically. This has led to a delay in presenting legislation that provides equal protection for the preborn baby. For Christians to use the "life of the mother" excuse and argue against bills of equal protection is unbiblical. It also demonstrates a gross misunderstanding or lack of comprehension of what an ectopic pregnancy is. I can't count how many well-meaning Christians have ectopic pregnancies as their excuse as to why a "life of the mother" exception is needed in legislation. What they often don't realize is that in their well-meaning aim to be considerate of the reality of ectopic

---

[55] Cleveland Clinic, "Laparoscopic Surgery: Purpose, Procedure & What It Is," Cleveland Clinic, March 16, 2022, https://my.clevelandclinic.org/health/treatments/22552-laparoscopic-surgery.

[56] Mayo Clinic, "Ectopic Pregnancy - Diagnosis and Treatment - Mayo Clinic," Mayoclinic.org, May 12, 2022, https://www.mayoclinic.org/diseases-conditions/ectopic-pregnancy/diagnosis-treatment/drc-20372093.

pregnancies, they dismiss the reality that no ectopic pregnancy is dealt with in an abortion mill; all are treated in a qualified hospital.

Well-intentioned Christians, even pastors, who are arguing for a "life of the mother" exception to abortion are arguing for abortion to remain legal. Did you get that? Christian pastors are arguing for abortions (prenatal homicide) to remain legal. Often in their gross ignorance they inadvertently argue for abortion mills to stay open. In their gross misunderstanding and biblical ignorance, they distort the doctrine of equal standards of justice and strip away the foundation for understanding the perfect justice of God displayed in the substitutionary atonement.

There is no biblical defense for supporting the "life of the mother" exception, but unfortunately many pastors believe this to be acceptable counsel. Pastors, Christians, Legislators, this ought not be the case! Christians should never again fall for this horrendous argument that preys on biblical ignorance and medical incompetence.

Here is the biblically and medically consistent thing to do in the case of ectopic pregnancies:

1. Doctors should practice watchful waiting.
2. If necessary, treat both mother and baby to help baby implant safely.
3. As a last resort, premature delivery in the form of the aforementioned laparoscopic procedures.

As previously stated, in a vast majority of cases the baby is sadly already dead by the time there is acknowledgment of the pregnancy being ectopic or symptoms of an ectopic pregnancy are exhibited to the point of needing treatment. Also, it is pertinent to note that in most cases the pregnancy terminates in the form of a miscarriage and resolves on its own. Since ectopic pregnancies are rare, and ectopic pregnancies needing medical intervention are even more rare, it is crucial to note that, though important, this discussion is of the rare exceptions within the rare exceptions.

Friends, no ectopic pregnancy emergency is treated ethically by surgical abortion. For further study, please reference Appendix D where you will find an article from the Southern Baptists For Abolishing Abortion website. I highly commend it to you.

11

Where the Rubber Meets the Road

Now that you have all this biblical knowledge and insight into what abortion is and isn't, what do you do with it? In the book of James, James tells us that "faith without works is dead," (James 2:14-26) which means that those who claim to have faith in Jesus Christ but never live out that faith in action deceive themselves into believing they know Christ when, in fact, they do not. We must not be those who claim truth but never preach truth or live by it.

Theology devoid of action is merely academic head knowledge and not firmly rooted belief. The same can be said of those who understand the arguments laid out in this book. Those who claim to affirm the Doctrine of Equal Standards of Justice and yet never act on it deceive themselves and do not truly believe it.

May it not be the case with you. May you not merely look at the truth and deposit it for some debates online later, but rather let the conviction of God's Word drive you to biblically directed, righteous action. Here are some righteous action steps you could take:

Prayer and Fasting

Prayer on behalf of the preborn baby and the legislative process is vital, for we are not in a battle primarily against flesh and blood but against the spiritual forces in the heavenly realms. (Eph. 6:12) Nothing will happen without prayer. We will not see a movement of God apart from the faithful intercession of the saints of God. God chooses to act as a result of the faithful pleading of the saints according to His will. So yes, pray fervently! Pray for the expansion of the Gospel to the ends of the earth, and pray passionately and regularly for the end of abortion. Fast faithfully for the end of abortion. This can be done in long, deliberate fasting or regular fasting of a meal on a specific day while praying for the end of abortion. Remember, fasting doesn't have to be limited to food. There are many other things outside of food that you can fast from should you need to.

Share

Since you now know the truth, share the truth with as many people as you can. Have passionate but loving conversations with those in your spheres of influence. Be patient; not everyone will come on board right away. Some of us are a stubborn lot (I fell into this category). Every doctrinal conviction takes time. Therefore, we must approach this doctrine no differently. Pray for the changing of hearts, share the truth in love, and demonstrate the consistent witness of Scripture that supports the Doctrine of Equal Standards of Justice, not through cunning logical argumentation, but rather through biblical exegesis. It would also be great to see churches put an article in their statements of faith demonstrating a resolute stance on the Doctrine of Equal Standards of Justice.

Interpose

While there is, in some sense, overlap with all the aforementioned, this step is quintessentially what we think of when we think of action steps. Here is where you act on behalf of the preborn.

As a Christian who believes in the inerrancy of Scripture, I see it as fully trustworthy and reliable. However, that is not where I stop; I also believe in the sufficiency of Scripture, meaning I take Paul seriously in his letter to Timothy:

> You, however, have followed my teaching, my conduct, my aim in life, my faith, my patience, my love, my steadfastness, my persecutions and sufferings that happened to me at Antioch, at Iconium, and at Lystra—which persecutions I endured; yet from them all the Lord rescued me. Indeed, all who desire to live a godly life in Christ Jesus will be persecuted, while evil people and impostors will go on from bad to worse, deceiving and being deceived. But as for you, continue in what you have learned and have firmly believed, knowing from whom you learned it and how from childhood you have been acquainted with the sacred writings, which are able to make you wise for salvation through faith in Christ Jesus. All Scripture is breathed out by God and profitable for teaching, for reproof, for correction, and for training in righteousness, that the man of God may be complete, equipped for every good work. (2 Tim. 3:10-17)

This irrefutably illustrates God's righteous Word as the only means by which we are to confront the illogical lies of Satan. See, Paul is articulating to his young disciple that he himself was persecuted for holding firmly to the Word of God and preaching it. He writes that all who desire to live a godly life will be persecuted, and evil people will continue to progress in how evil they are and will continue to do evil. The admonition for young Timothy is not to fret the evil actions of the children of Satan, but rather to do what? To continue in what Paul has taught him, to hold firm to the faith he believed, and hold firm to the Scriptures from which it came to him. Paul states that the Scriptures are able to make one wise for salvation through faith in Christ Jesus. Then he declares what the Scriptures are. In that declaration, does he state they are mere suggestions to be taken or left when we think it might not help our position? Not at all. "All Scripture is breathed out by God and profitable for teaching, for reproof, for correction, and for training in righteousness, that the man of God may be complete, equipped for every good work." (2 Tim. 3:16-17) It seems that the position of Paul is that our marching orders must be derived from Scripture. There is no area of life that is not addressed by the righteous, perfect Word of God. We cannot rightly interpose if we neglect God's Word as our standard for righteous action.

Although standing for our preborn neighbor with biblical conviction is righteous, standing on behalf of our preborn neighbor primarily guided by pragmatic planning and philosophical convictions is misdirected. Pragmatism always leads to being a hindrance in this fight.

With this in mind, interposing on behalf of the preborn baby can take many forms. Giving and going are the most common forms.

Giving

Financially funding righteous organizations or people who are interposing physically on behalf of the preborn according to Scripture is a huge and necessary help in this fight. Groups like End Abortion Ohio,[57] Abolitionists Rising,[58] Liberty Rising Institute,[59] Southern Baptists For Abolishing

---

[57] End Abortion Ohio, "Who We Are," Endabortionohio.com, 2022, https://www.endabortionohio.com/about.

[58] Abolitionists Rising, "Who We Are," abolitionistsrising.com, December 7, 2021, https://abolitionistsrising.com/about.

[59] Liberty Rising Institute, "Our Mission," Liberty Rising Institute, 2021, https://www.liberty-rising.org/#mission.

Abortion,[60] Rescue Those,[61] Abolish Abortion Florida,[62] Abolish Abortion Oklahoma,[63] End Abortion Now,[64] Abolish Abortion Texas,[65] Action For Life,[66] and an ever-growing list of many others all need financial help in this fight.

Going God's Way

Going can look like prayerfully, biblically, and purposely pleading on behalf of the preborn baby at the abortion clinic. This must be done, however, with honesty and the glory of God as the goal. If we lose track of this, then in the fray we will look just like the world. While it might be tempting to use tricks or dishonesty, doing so reveals a small view of God. We do not need to resort to dishonest schemes to rescue babies. We must unapologetically condemn abortion, preach the Gospel, and call the sinners to repent and turn to Christ. Our scheming will not change the murderous-minded sinner's heart; rather, God is the One who authored the number of their days. Doing what is evil never truly pays off, even if the motives for said evil actions are good.

Light bearers don't resort to darkness to bring about the light, but rather remember that they are set apart to shine. Shining is tiresome, often

---

[60] Southern Baptists For Abolishing Abortion, "Who Are We?," Southern Baptists for Abolishing Abortion, May 30, 2020, https://southernbaptistsabolishingabortion.com/about/.

[61] Rescue Those, "What Must I Do?," Rescuethose.com, 2021, https://www.rescuethose.com/media/.

[62] Abolish Abortion Florida, "We, the People of Florida, Demand Equal Protection & Equal Justice," Abolish Abortion Florida, n.d., https://www.abolishabortionflorida.com/.

[63] Abolish Abortion Oklahoma, "About," Abolish Abortion Oklahoma, n.d., https://abolishabortionok.org/about/.

[64] End Abortion Now, "Who We Are," End Abortion Now, November 11, 2022, https://endabortionnow.com/who-we-are/.

[65] Abolish Abortion Texas, "Who We Are," Abolish Abortion Texas, 2016, https://abolishabortiontx.org/our-history/.

[66] Action For Life, "About AFL," Action For Life, 2020, https://www.takeactionforlife.org/about-afl.

undervalued, and rarely, if ever, is applauded by the world. Remember, though, that turning off the light only ever amplifies the darkness. Biblically responding to abortion must mean responding in a way that is consistent with Scripture. We cannot manufacture results; we can, however, pray for the strength to be biblically faithful and consistent regardless of the perceived effectiveness of our ministry.

Going can also look like advocating for your church to get involved in this fight against abortion. This, too, will take time and patience. No amount of berating those who aren't quite there yet will get them to join you. Pray for them and lead them to the truth with love. Develop real relationships with church members, and inevitably you will see brothers and sisters in Christ get on board because they will respect your conviction on this issue. If you are not committed to the local body of Christ, you have no place attempting to start a ministry at the abortion clinic near you. You need both the accountability and support to continue this type of ministry.

Finally, going is also meeting with and urging your legislator to act in his capacity as a lesser magistrate to protect life by sponsoring a bill of equal protection. Much of the same could be said about this section as the previous section on going to the abortion clinics. You cannot be a lone ranger in ministry and be a healthy Christian. All the earlier aforementioned organizations would be great places to start your "going" process after sitting down with your local church elders and those who know you well to explain your convictions and desire to do this ministry. Many ministries won't even let you be involved unless you have the blessing of your church leaders. If you think that a legislator will take you seriously without a network of individuals and church members supporting you, you are sorely mistaken. I highly recommend inviting your elders to join you at your meetings with the legislators.

Run

You may be one who needs to consider running to be a legislator. However, we must be wise about who we have run for legislative office because not everyone should. If you feel the Lord is leading you in this direction, don't make this decision in a vacuum. It is vitally important to pray, seek wise counsel from your local church elders, and get training from a group like Liberty Rising Institute. Just like any other pursuit in life, we want to honor Jesus Christ in all we do. This necessarily means that we must not be half committed; we must be well-studied and show ourselves ready for the task. If you are not fully committed to running with all you have, DO NOT RUN!

Unfortunately, there are many men who half-heartedly run and seek the title of candidate as a badge of honor. We do not need these types of men in the fight, for they make a mockery of our cause and a mockery of our God. We need serious and qualified men to step into this gap, ready for war, because the burden of the lesser magistrate is a great one. Realistically, you cannot be a one-issue candidate and win. Though your primary reason for running can be to bring forward a bill of equal protection, you need to have well-developed, biblically informed positions on many other important issues ranging from combating the encroachment of transgenderism and the new moral sexual revolution to economic policy. We need statesmen directed by biblical conviction and principle, not pragmatically guided inferences and political wind-checking.

All Hands on Deck

Regardless of where you are able to contribute to this fight, we need you. Whether that be through prayer, financial support, educating others, activism on the street, interposing outside the abortion mills, lobbying, or running for legislative office, we need you in this fight. We cannot continue to be silent as millions of our preborn neighbors are murdered. Apathy toward the plight of preborn image-bearers of God is an affirmation of their oppression, and it is sinful! We must all take biblically directed and decisive action.

12

A Letter to the Christian Legislator

"It is not only because the gradual Abolitionists have been, in fact, the only real stay of that system of wickedness and cruelty which we wish to abolish; though that assertion is unquestionably true; but it is trying beyond expression that they should be the real maintainers of the Slave Trade."
-William Wilberforce[67]

The following is a letter for the person currently holding an office in local, state, or federal government. Though this letter is good for everyone to read and pass on to their legislators, this is written for the legislator.

Dear Christian Legislator,

Thank you for taking seriously your God-given responsibility as a lesser magistrate in office. I addressed you earlier in this book, but hopefully at this point in the reading, you thoroughly understand that, as a Christian, your response must be to stand for the preborn; not in vague, politically feasible ways, but rather in sacrificial, urgent ways.

Sadly, today there is a scarcity of principle in politics, as I am sure you are all too familiar with. Too many legislators are more concerned with being politically feasible rather than biblically faithful. There are too many

---

[67] William Wilberforce, *A Letter on the Abolition of the Slave Trade*, 1807, 295.

legislators who neglect the urgency to act on biblical conviction and principle.

Thank you for seeking to know and understand the biblical response to prenatal homicide. You have read the arguments and had the opportunity to see the biblical claims; will you interpose on behalf of your preborn neighbor God's way?

I hope you find the information in this book to be a helpful tool and supplement to your regular study of God's Word as you fight for the preborn baby. Once you understand the fundamentals of the doctrine of Equal Standards of Justice, it's impossible to sustain consistency with Scripture while arguing against God's standard of justice by compromising that standard legislatively with things like Heartbeat Bills or bills that do not criminalize the act of preborn homicide. We must seek to hold everyone culpable accountable with criminal legal action; all this after due process has taken place, of course. It is only then that God is glorified and will bless our efforts.

God's way is rarely politically feasible and rarely costs you nothing of your political capital. In fact, it may cost you everything. However, God's way is just. For the Christian, following God's way is the necessary precondition to acting faithfully in the very position of influence that God has given you. Are you ready to engage the culture with the Gospel, Christian legislator? Then stand firm on principle and let your "yes" be yes and your "no" be no; it is as simple as that. We are exhorted to do this by Jesus Himself in Matthew 5:37 and also told that to do otherwise is from the evil one. Are you being played by Satan or unapologetically serving Christ in office? I pray it is the latter! If not, it's not too late to redirect your efforts to risk your political career for Jesus. After all, it is the Lord who holds the hearts of kings in His hand, and Scripture tells us they are like water in his hands. (Pro. 21:1)

Who is Lord? I pray for you that it is King Jesus! May the peace of God, found only in Christ Jesus, be with you and those you love. May He grant rest to your eyes at night, but if you neglect His holy standard of justice, may He not let rest come to you until you repent and work tirelessly for Equal Protection and Equal Justice for the preborn.

Thank you for reading this!

Sincerely,

Mike Harding

(just a nobody serving the greatest of somebodies, King Jesus, and may He alone get the praise!)

13

Conclusion

There is always more that could be said, but like a good sermon this plane should land. Let me wrap up by summarizing.

Abortion is a grievous evil staining our land, and the church must respond with a biblically consistent answer to this atrocity. The silence of the church at large on this issue is condemnation requiring repentance from us all. No amount of donating to abortion ministries like pregnancy resource centers (though they are necessary) or sidewalk advocacy groups outside abortion mills will end this atrocity. Don't get me wrong, these are necessary bandages to stop the bloodletting. In fact, they work in conjunction with each other. However, they are bandages that cannot cure the greater problem. The problem, as Pastor Bill Ascol so wisely states it, "is a heart problem." There is only One who changes hearts, and without the work of the Spirit of God in the heart of sinful man, there is no redemption of that man. Repentance is a fruit of regeneration having taken place. We don't manufacture our will out of thin air to repent. God grants us the fruit of regeneration which is repentance.

Pastors will need to be willing to lose the seeker-sensitive tribe in their churches. They must be prepared to be publicly ostracized, gaslighted, and/or threatened for the sake of the preborn neighbor. However, the thunderous sound of biblically consistent preaching on God's answer to child sacrifice could be, and one day will be, deafening to our enemies, not damning silence!

CONCLUSION

Woe to the men and women who know the right thing to do in this critical moment while faced with this grave evil and fail to do it! Woe to the legislator who cowers in the face of men versus the face of God!

Take courage in Christ, Christian, and resolve to bleed with the faithful as we bring the Gospel in conflict with our culture and demand that the mass murdering of the preborn among us cease. We must, with a loud and unified voice, demand that the bloodletting and sacrifices of preborn image bearers of God stop immediately.

Appendix A - "Answers to Abortion Arguments" by Joel Beeke

What is the justification for legal abortion? Let us examine the arguments used by those who promote abortion to determine on how strong of a foundation this practice is based.

Arguments for Abortion

Argument 1: The fetus is not a human life, therefore it may be killed.

While the fetus will eventually become a human child, this argument says it is not yet so. But science indicates otherwise. First, the words "embryo" and "fetus" are Greek and Latin words which simply mean "young one." When scientists speak of a human embryo or fetus, they are not putting it in the category of another species, but are simply using technical terminology for a stage of development, like the words infant, child, adolescent, and adult. A human fetus is a young human person in the womb. It is natural and correct for mothers to speak of the fetus as "my baby" or for pregnancy books to say "your child."

Second, from conception the child has its own genetic code which clearly identifies it as *homo sapiens* – part of the human race. The child's DNA also has a distinct code from the mother, showing that he or she is not a part of her body, but a distinct individual living temporarily within her.

Third, ultrasound imaging shows that very early in the process of development the embryo grows into a recognizable human form. The child is not a blob of tissue, but a highly complex, though tiny, baby. At three weeks after conception a baby's heart begins beating and pumping blood through the body. At six weeks a baby's brain waves are traceable. Virtually all surgical abortions silence a beating heart and a functioning brain. At eight weeks the arms, hands, legs, and feet are well developed and the child's fingerprints are starting to form. At eleven weeks after conception all of the baby's internal organs are present and functioning. By the end of the first trimester, the baby kicks, spins, somersaults, opens and closes hands, and makes facial expressions.

By any reasonable standard, a human fetus is a young human being. To kill an innocent baby is murder. That's why the products of abortion are so ugly: severed hands, feet, and heads wrapped up in bags and discarded. On an intuitive level, we know this. People can shrug off the image of a side of beef or a chicken drumstick, but images of abortion horrify and grieve us because they are images of a dismembered human body. Unborn children are precious human beings and must be protected.

Argument 2: The fetus is not fully human because it is dependent on another.

Is a baby kangaroo not a kangaroo because it lives in its mother pouch? Of course not. The location and situation of a human being does not make him or her any less human. Arguments for abortion based on dependence tread on dangerous ground. If dependency makes a person less human, then on that ground we would have the right to kill infants outside the womb, people on dialysis, handicapped people, and the elderly. May we kill all dependent people?

Consider two mothers several months into their pregnancies. One child is born prematurely, and the other remains in the womb. The first is utterly dependent on medical intervention to survive, and the other on her mother's body. Is it right to kill the prematurely born baby? How would the hospital staff react if the mother entered the neonatal ward with a knife to attack her child? If it is not right to kill the premature child, then why is it right to kill the child in the womb? Both are dependent. Both are children. Both must have legal protection.

Argument 3: A woman has a right to do with her body as she desires.

We affirm a woman's authority over her body. But there are limits to what we can rightfully do with our bodies, including causing harm to another human being. Abortion involves the death of her child. To argue that the living fetus is part of the mother's body defies reason: which organ of her body is it? When the unborn child's heart beats, whose heart is it? When the fetus's brain waves can be traced, whose brain is it? Every pregnancy involves two people, a mother and a child; the rights of both must be considered.

Whenever we speak of the rights of two human beings, we must guard against the more powerful person taking advantage of the weaker person. It is the responsibility of the powerful to protect the weak. It is especially the responsibility of a mother to protect her child. Does any mother have the right to do whatever she pleases with her children? On the contrary, she has the responsibility of caring for them or seeing that someone else cares for them. Certainly motherhood calls for sacrifice. We should expect adults to make sacrifices of their resources and freedoms when necessary to preserve the lives of children.

Argument 4: Sex and reproduction are private matters into which we must not intrude.

We believe that human sexuality is a very private matter; it expresses the deep intimacy that a husband and wife share. But sex has very public consequences. How we exercise our sexuality contributes to the restraint or spread of disease, the treatment of women with honor or rape, the nurture or sexual abuse of children, and the strengthening or dissolution of families which are the foundation of society. Society therefore has a compelling interest to guard the dignity of marriage, women, and children with respect to sex and reproduction.

People sometimes argue that the U.S. Constitution guarantees the right to privacy in sexual and reproductive matters. Read the Constitution, and you will not find any such right there. In reality, the Fourth Amendment acknowledges the right of security against *"unreasonable searches and seizures"* without a *"warrant,"* but says nothing about sexuality, children, or abortion.

Someone might sarcastically say, "I thought what I did in my bedroom was my own business." But if there is reasonable cause to believe that you are murdering a child in your bedroom, then it becomes a matter of public intervention by the authorities. Privacy is not an absolute moral right. But killing a child is an absolute moral wrong.

Argument 5: Making abortion illegal would force women into dangerous, back-alley abortions.

The idea of the crudely done abortion resulting in a bleeding, dying mother (and a dead child) has been widely used by abortion advocates. But in reality, 90 percent of abortions performed before they became legal were done by physicians in their offices. The idea of thousands of women dying yearly until abortion was legalized is a myth. In 1972 only thirty-nine mothers died in the United States from abortions. The *American Journal of Obstetrics and Gynecology* (March 26, 2010) admits that the legalization of abortion has had *"no major impact on the number of women dying from abortion in the U.S. ... legal abortion is now the leading cause of abortion-related maternal deaths in the U.S."*

Every woman who dies from a botched abortion is a tragic loss. But so is every child who dies from a successful abortion. We should not make it legal to kill babies in order to make the killing safer for the adults involved. Furthermore, abortion has medical and psychological risks; making it illegal would actually protect the lives and health of millions of women.

Argument 6: Better to die before birth than to live as an unwanted child.

First, to give a human being the power to determine the future life of another individual based on whether he is "wanted" or "unwanted" is most dangerous. Do we have the right to kill people based on whether or not we want them? Such a viewpoint leads highly cultured societies to commit genocide against the mentally challenged and "inferior" races.

Second, is the child never wanted by anyone? Many mothers did not want the pregnancy but cherish the child, especially after birth. There are also many parents who want to adopt a child. To say that the child is not wanted now by its mother does not mean it will never be loved.

Third, this argument has horrifying implications for "unwanted" children already born. If it is better to kill the baby than to let it be unwanted, then what does that imply about homeless children? Children with abusive parents? Would it be loving to kill these children? Of course not; love calls us to teach their parents to care for them or to find parents for them. In the same way, if unborn children are truly "unwanted," we should try to help their mothers to see them differently, or help the children to find adoptive parents. Did you know that Steve Jobs was unwanted by his birth mother and the adopting parents the government initially chose?

Fourth, what gives us the right to decide whether it is better for a person to live or to die? Are we the owner of that person's life? Do we know the child's future for certain? Do not many "unwanted" children overcome severe physical or emotional handicaps in their youth and function as useful adult citizens? Do not many people in painful situations nevertheless wisely choose to live rather than to kill themselves?

In the end, the seemingly compassionate argument for the "wanted" child makes no sense at all. At best it is an emotional, illogical appeal; at worst it is a mask for deadly selfishness.

Argument 7: Pro-life advocates are trying to force their beliefs on other people.

In reality, all who participate in an abortion force their views on another, namely on the unborn child – so strongly in fact, that it results in his or her death. If the unborn child is a human being, then how can one be accused of trying to force his own belief on another when trying to protect the life of the child from his or her killer? If the unborn child is a human being, then abortion is *murder*. If abortion is murder we must do all in our power to stop it.

The Declaration of Independence says,

> We hold these truths to be self-evident, that all men are created equal, that they are endowed by their Creator with certain unalienable rights, that among these are life, liberty and the pursuit of happiness – that to secure these rights, governments are instituted among men, deriving their just powers from the consent of the governed.

Currently the rights of some people are more "equal" than others, because their *"liberty and the pursuit of happiness"* apparently justifies taking the "life" of others. This seriously undermines the political foundation of our nation. But if people exercise their popular power of voting to direct the government to protect all people's right to life, they simply do what the Declaration of Independence says they should.

After critically examining seven basic arguments for abortion upon demand, can we honestly conclude on a rational and ethical basis that abortion should be legal? These arguments are flimsy reasons for murdering more than a million babies each year. This is especially evident when we consider that less than 5% of all abortions are for reasons of rape, incest, or a danger to the mother's life. More than 95% of abortions take place for the sake of finances, career, personal convenience, or other selfish reasons. Are these compelling reasons for killing human beings?

Joel Beeke, "Answers to Abortion Arguments," in *Abortion* (Pensacola, FL: Chapel Library, 2012), 22-26.

Appendix B - A Biblical Resolution for the Abolition of All Abortions in Ohio

This resolution was written for, presented at, and passed during the State Convention of Baptists in Ohio (SCBO) Annual Meeting held in November 2021.

WHEREAS, the confessional statement of Southern Baptists, The Baptist Faith and Message 2000, in Article XV, affirms that children, "from the moment of conception, are a blessing and heritage from the Lord" and further affirms that Southern Baptists are mandated by Scripture to "speak on behalf of the unborn and contend for the sanctity of all human life from conception to natural death"; and,

WHEREAS, the unborn are not second class image bearers of God but are from the moment of fertilization full image bearers of God, and we believe that humans are created in God's image by, through, and for Jesus to the glory of God, as Scripture declares that all souls belong to Him (Genesis 1:27; 4:1; 21:2; Isaiah 7:14; Colossians 1:16; Romans 11:36; Ezekiel 18:4), and all humans display objective worth before God, not varying on the basis of incidental characteristics such as ethnicity, age, size, circumstances of conception, mental development, physical development, manhood or womanhood, potential, or contribution to society (Romans 1:19-20; Genesis 1:27; 9:6; Matthew 18:6); and,

WHEREAS, the premeditated murder of any preborn image bearer of God is a sin, violating both the natural law of retributive justice as set forth in the Noahic covenant, as well as the sixth commandment forbidding murder, and as such, is ultimately an assault on God's image, seeking to usurp God's sovereignty as Creator (Genesis 9:5-6; Exodus 20:13; Proverbs 6:17); and,

WHEREAS, God establishes all governing authorities as His avenging servants to carry out His wrath on the evildoer and commands these authorities to judge justly, neither showing partiality to the wicked nor using unequal standards, which are abominations to God (Psalm 82; Proverbs 20:10; Romans 13:4); and

WHEREAS, in 1973, the Supreme Court of the United States attempted to usurp God's sovereignty and His law and rendered an iniquitous decision on Roe v. Wade, resulting in more than 63 million abortions in the United States since that time (Isaiah 5:23; 10:1-2; Psalm 2; Matthew 22:21; John 19:11; Acts 4:19; 5:29, Romans 13:1); therefore, be it,

RESOLVED, that the messengers of the 68th Annual Celebration of the State Convention of Baptists in Ohio, committed to the Word of God as our final authority on all matters of life and practice, do hereby state unequivocally that abortion is murder of an image bearer of God, and we reject any position that allows for any exceptions to God's perfect standard of justice (Psalm 94:6; Isaiah 10:1-2; Proverbs 24:11; Psalm 82:1-4); and be it further,

RESOLVED, that Ohio Baptists humbly confess, lament, and repent of any apathy to the sin of the murder of the preborn; and be it further,

RESOLVED, that we, without reservation, support our local pregnancy centers that do amazing work on behalf of the unborn, their parents, the post-abortive, and everyone affected by abortion; and be it further,

RESOLVED, that we affirm that redemption is available through Jesus Christ, including to those who have had an abortion or are complicit in abortion; and be it further,

RESOLVED, that, as the State Convention of Baptists in Ohio, we will engage in establishing equal protection and equal justice for the preborn by calling upon all governing authorities to use their positions to abolish abortion while protecting the life of the mother from imminent death in a life-threatening medical emergency to protect the rights of the unborn from conception; and be it finally,

RESOLVED, that we call on all pastors and ministry leaders to lead us to seek the complete and immediate abolition of abortion.

Appendix C - A Biblical Argument for Equal Protection in Ohio

Every human being, both inside and outside of their mother's womb, is an image bearer of God from fertilization. (Genesis 1:26-28, 5:1-2, 9:6; Romans 11:36, 1 Corinthians 11:7; James 3:9)

God's word demands that we love our neighbor as ourselves. (Leviticus 19:18; Matthew 19:19; Matthew 22:37-39; Mark 12:30-31; Luke 10:27; Romans 13:9; Galatians 5:14; James 2:8)

Every preborn baby is a person, a gift from God, and our neighbor. (Genesis 16:11, 25:21-22; Psalm 127:3-5; Psalm 139:13-16; Jeremiah 1:5; Luke 1:44)

Failing to provide equal protection and equal justice for any person is using unequal weights and measures and God calls this heinous act an abomination. (Proverbs 11:1;16:11; 20:10, 23; 29:7)

An average of more than 20,000 babies are ruthlessly murdered in their mothers' wombs in the state of Ohio each year. Their murderers face no repercussions. They walk with legal impunity. (Exodus 20:13, 21:22-25; Proverbs 24:11-12; Romans 13:1-14; Revelation 21:8)

We are commanded by Scripture to protect the fatherless and use equal weights and measures in our judgments. (Proverbs 11:1;16:11; 20:10, 23; 29:7; Isaiah 1:17; Micah 6:8-14; James 1:27)

The only biblical answer to abortion is Equal Protection and Equal justice for the preborn baby which necessitates criminalization. This merely means that we provide the same protections and due process in the law for the preborn baby as we do for any other born person. Until we do so, we are, by our lack of action or wrongly directed action, practicing ageism and gross negligence of our duties as Christians. (Genesis 9:6, Deuteronomy 25:13-16;

Leviticus 19:15; Leviticus 19:35-36; Proverbs 24:24-25; Ezekiel 45:9-10; Amos 5:24; Zechariah 7:9)

Appendix D - "What About Ectopic Pregnancies?" by Dusty Deevers

There are rare times in a pregnancy when the child is growing in the mother's body somewhere other than the womb, for example, in the fallopian tube, abdominal cavity, and very rarely inside one of her ovaries. Typically, doctors consider these pregnancies fatal so abortion is the prescribed solution. "It's better to save the mother by aborting the unborn child than to do nothing and allow both of them to die," they say. Studies show that not all, not even most, ectopic pregnancies threaten the life of the mother. However, many result in the death of the child. How do abolition bills deal with these types of situations? Is the mother, the doctor, or both liable for the murder of the child?

Abolition Bills and Ectopics

Abolition bills give mothers and doctors with no intention of killing a preborn child the confidence that the law will protect *them* as equally as it protects the *baby*. Abolition bills recognize and establish that life begins at fertilization/conception and provides preborn humans from that point onward with the same legal protections against murder as anyone else. They assert due process and equal protection under the law.

Here is the exact language of Senate Bill 13, an abolition bill in Oklahoma.

> "It is the intent of the Legislature to provide to unborn children the equal protection of the laws of this state; to establish that a living human child, from the moment of fertilization upon the fusion of a

human spermatozoon with a human ovum, is entitled to the same rights, powers, privileges, justice, and protections as are secured or granted by the laws of the state to any other human person."

Consider the language of Section 16-3-107 of the proposed abolition bill in South Carolina named, "South Carolina Prenatal Equal Protection Act of 2023." This section deals with ectopics.

> (A) Medical care or treatment provided with the requisite consent by a licensed physician to avert the death of a pregnant woman that results in the accidental or unintentional injury or death of her unborn child when all reasonable alternatives to save the life of the unborn child were attempted or none were available does not constitute a violation of this article.
>
> (B) Mistake or unintentional error on the part of a licensed physician or other licensed health care provider or his or her employee or agent or any person acting on behalf of the patient shall not subject the licensed physician or other licensed health care provider or person acting on behalf of the patient to any criminal liability under this article.
>
> (C) Medical care or treatment includes, but is not limited to, ordering, dispensation, or administration of prescribed medications and medical procedures.

Attorney Bradley Pierce, of the Foundation to Abolish Abortion, offers the following explanation of this section in his drafter's notes. Medical care or treatment provided with the requisite consent by a licensed physician to avert the death of a pregnant female that results in the accidental or unintentional injury or death of her unborn child is not a crime when all reasonable alternatives to save the life of the unborn child were attempted or none were unavailable.

Some might call this a "life of the mother" provision. For example, this language would allow a physician to treat a life-threatening ectopic pregnancy.

It is important to point out that this is not an abortion "exception." The common non-medical meaning of the term abortion is the intentional destruction of a fetus. In this instance, the death of the preborn child is an un-intended result of a treatment used as a last resort to avert the death of the mother.

It is important to note that the bill does not allow for direct abortion but only allows for the "unintentional" death of the child in these specific circumstances. Therefore, for example, it does not allow for the use of methotrexate to intentionally cause the death of the child. This is in agreement with the Dublin Declaration. Further, Subsection (B) clarifies that health care providers, etc. cannot be prosecuted for mistakes or other unintentional errors.

Southern Baptists for Abolishing Abortion is in agreement with Attorney Pierce.

Abolition bills promote proper life-saving intervention and intention, and deter murderous intervention and intention. In the event, of last resort, that doctors intervene and exhaust their ability to save the life, and the child dies, they performed medical triage and before the law of God and man can stand justified in their actions with a clear conscience.

Ectopic and Medical Necessity Keys

Ectopic pregnancies are a tragedy during which medical triage is necessary, with doctors never ceasing to treat both mother and baby as human beings and upholding the Hippocratic Oath by exhausting all possible options to save as many human lives as they can. We affirm the conclusions of the Dublin Declaration stating that, "direct abortion is not medically necessary to save the life of a woman" and that "the prohibition of abortion does not affect, in any way, the availability of optimal care to pregnant women."

We deny that treatment for miscarriages and ectopic pregnancies are murder by abortion. The predominant number of babies that implant somewhere other than the uterus pass away before any treatment is given. Removal of a deceased baby is not abortion. In cases of surviving ectopics, we must not equivocate between preterm delivery (leading to the unintended and inevitable death of the baby) and the intentional destruction of the baby by abortion through Dilation and Evacuation (D&E) or Dilation and Curettage (D&C). This conflation of preterm delivery with intentional destruction also impugns grieving parents who are forced to deliver the child early.

Further, we must press for doctors to utilize medical advancements, such as those found in *in vitro* fertilization (IVF), for relocation and implantation of an embryo in an ectopic pregnancy.

First, the approach in true healthcare, under the Hippocratic Oath, is "do no harm." Meaning: do everything you can to save a life. Abortionists are not aiming to save a life. On the contrary, they are aiming to take life. In the situation of ectopic pregnancy and a living baby, a doctor would have two patients, mother and baby, with both of their well being in mind.

Second, an ectopic pregnancy is an emergency situation that should be managed and monitored in a hospital emergency room, not an abortion clinic. Abortion clinics schedule their life-taking murders in advance. Emergency rooms provide life-saving care immediately.

Third, if the doctor is doing everything he/she can to save both lives, his/her training in medical triage will assist him/her in providing care. Should the baby die in the process of trying to save both lives, then just as in any other triage situation, he/she is neither a murderer nor held liable as such. He/she neither had the intent to murder nor the ability ultimately to save the life he/she was trying to save. Like any other healthcare law affecting doctors, abolition bills would not punish a well-meaning doctor for trying to save a life.

Fourth, all states already have laws on record, which would still be in effect with the passage of an abolition bill, protecting doctors from prosecution if they "make a good faith effort to save the life of a patient, but are unable to do so."

Fifth, a mother whose intention is to do all she can to save and not kill her baby is both not a murderer, nor will she be held responsible for her baby's death in an ectopic pregnancy she could not control, or the doctor could not save.

Sixth, each state's homicide laws, which would be the enforcement mechanism in the event an abolition bill was passed, would not punish a mother or a doctor for attempting to do all they could to save the life of the baby.

Abortion Exceptions and Loopholes

What's further, if a Pro-Life bill leaves an *abortion* exception for the "life of the mother" or any other loophole, it will be abused. An exception for ectopic pregnancies to be treated and given the full range of care is not necessary. The presence of a life of the mother exception for an abortion in an abolition bill would only serve as an unnecessary loophole. Abolition bills make no exception for ectopic abortion, because there should be no such thing as a doctor who intervenes with the intention to kill a child.

Caring for ectopic pregnancy is not abortion.

Language allowing an abortion procedure to save the life of the mother is unnecessary because:

1. Treating ectopic pregnancies is not D&E or D&C abortion.
2. Our current homicide laws already sort out these situations to serve justice for the victim and punishment for the criminal; and,
3. Doctors are already operating under the Hippocratic Oath and daily making professional decisions just like this when treating multiple patients at once and triaging. Under true healthcare, the doctor's intent isn't to take a life. It is to save all he can. He is not criminalized for doing that now and won't be under an abolition bill. An abolition bill would serve to send the death of the baby into the currently applicable investigatory processes and laws, whether by the hospital, law enforcement, or both.

Language addressing the life of the mother also allows for too many exceptions because:

1. It is unnecessary to add exemptions to current laws dealing with culpability in homicides,
2. If you add that language, you make exceptions for justice and equal protection under the law. As was said before, doctors do not need exceptions for providing life-saving care. Provide health care without the intent to take a life. If it happens in the process of having to save the mother, under an ectopic, it is no different than other triage situations with multiple critical patients. Exceptions are loopholes abortion-minded doctors and mothers will exploit.

Expectant Management: Three Options

"Expectant Management" of high-risk pregnancies applies to cases in which the doctor monitors the pregnancy closely but does not administer any direct treatment." In cases of ectopic pregnancy or other situations that present potential threats to the physical health of the mother, the pregnancy is carried until one of three actions take place:

1. **Self-resolution**: For ectopic pregnancy, this means spontaneous migration of the baby (*fetus*) to a viable location, or miscarriage.
2. **Inducement & Delivery**: If self-resolution does not take place, and the baby is alive (viable), then labor is induced and livesaving measures are administered to the child, and mother, if needed, so that both mom and baby survive, or
3. **Surgical Delivery**: The pregnancy presents an immediate threat to the life of the child, mother, or both, at which point either labor is induced, or surgery is performed. The child is born, not dismembered through abortion. The child may very well not survive, and while this would be a tragedy, it would not be intentional murder. This procedure is performed in a hospital under doctors, not scheduled in an abortuary.

In any case, abortion is never medically necessary. The abolitionist affirms the Hippocratic Oath and believes that the life of the mother and the life of the child are equally valuable, and should be afforded equal protection, dignity, and respect. Public policy and medical treatment should also reflect that reality.

Dusty Deevers, "What about Ectopic Pregnancies?," Southern Baptists for Abolishing Abortion, June 10, 2020, https://southernbaptistsabolishingabortion.com/2020/06/10/what-about-ectopic-pregnancies/.

Appendix E - Dublin Declaration on Maternal Healthcare

As experienced practitioners and researchers in obstetrics and gynaecology, we affirm that direct abortion – the purposeful destruction of the unborn child – is not medically necessary to save the life of a woman.

We uphold that there is a fundamental difference between abortion, and necessary medical treatments that are carried out to save the life of the mother, even if such treatment results in the loss of life of her unborn child.

We confirm that the prohibition of abortion does not affect, in any way, the availability of optimal care to pregnant women.

Committee on Excellence in Maternal Healthcare, "Dublin Declaration on Maternal Healthcare," Dublin Declaration, September 2012, http://www.dublindeclaration.com/translations/.

About the Author

Michael Harding, also known as Mike, is an unashamed follower of Jesus Christ. He is husband to Emily, father to Joanna and Hannah on this side of heaven, and father to Sam, whose time on earth in Mommy's belly was short but cherished. Mike spent 9 years serving in the Army National Guard and is a 2009-2010 Operation Iraqi Freedom veteran. He previously had the honor of serving as a youth pastor in Sandia Park, NM, and later as a senior pastor in Millersburg, OH. He is committed to seeing the practice of slaughtering preborn image bearers of God abolished once and for all.

You can connect with me on:
- https://twitter.com/MikeRCM1988
- https://facebook.com/mande0728

Also by Michael Harding

35 Days in Paul's Letter to the Philippian Church
Are you looking for a resource to help jump start a quiet time with Jesus? Do you find yourself wondering what book of the Bible to read or how to read the word of God? Michael Harding has provided a resource that is aimed at doing all of the above. If you will commit to just 35 days in the letter that the Apostle Paul wrote to the church in Philippi, you will be challenged to reflect Christ in all areas of your life.

Made in the USA
Columbia, SC
08 August 2024